These days, cooking at home is a top priority for beloved chef and TV host Chuck Hughes. Compared to the hectic pace of his restaurant—where cooking on the line requires lightning speed and expert precision—cooking at home is all about taking things slow, having a good playlist, and knowing a few sure-fire techniques to make meals quick and easy, especially during those busy weekdays.

Chuck's Home Cooking features Chuck's favourite go-to recipes to cook for his family, whether it's an easy weeknight dinner, a delicious weekend treat, or a dish to impress on special occasions. One thing is for sure: they're all on steady rotation in Chuck's home. Juggling work and a young family, Chuck knows first-hand that the hustle of everyday daily life can make mealtime feel like a chore—but with his simple planning and prep-ahead methods, delicious dishes with bold flavours come together with ease!

Inside you'll find quick-and-delicious recipes to start the day; easy to make every day breads including biscuits, loaves, and bagels; soups and stews; pastas; make-your-own pizza dough along with Chuck's favourite pizza recipes; and mouthwatering desserts. Packed with plenty of dishes for dinners, including Fried Chicken with Hot Pepper Maple Glaze; Boiled Chicken Stew with Dumplings; Meat Pie with Fruit Ketchup; Braised Beef Short Ribs; Sausage and Pepperoni Lasagna; Swordfish Kebobs; and Fish Burgers. *Chuck's Home Cooking* is a celebration of cooking at home, rich with Chuck's favourite family recipes, seasonal classics, and even a cabane à sucre (sugar shack) feast.

Chuck's Home Cooking

Chuck's Home Cooking

Family-Favourite Recipes from My Kitchen to Yours

Chuck Hughes

PENGUIN

an imprint of Penguin Canada, a division of Penguin Random House Canada Limited

Canada • USA • UK • Ireland • Australia • New Zealand • India • South Africa • China

First published 2024

www.penguinrandomhouse.ca

LIBRARY AND ARCHIVES CANADA CATALOGUING IN PUBLICATION

Title: Chuck's home cooking : family-favourite recipes from my kitchen to yours / Chuck Hughes.
Names: Hughes, Chuck, 1976- author.
Description: Includes index.
Identifiers: Canadiana (print) 20230557430 | Canadiana (ebook) 20230557449 |
ISBN 9780735243668 (hardcover) | ISBN 9780735243675 (EPUB)
Subjects: LCSH: Cooking. | LCSH: Quick and easy cooking. | LCGFT: Cookbooks.
Classification: LCC TX714 .H843 2024 | DDC 641.5—dc23

Cover and interior design by Andrew Roberts
Typeset by Terra Page
Cover and interior photography by Marc-André Lavoie
Food and prop styling by Chuck Hughes and Christopher Merrick

Printed in China

10 9 8 7 6 5 4 3 2 1

To my kids, Charlie and Henri

Contents

Introduction

First, THANK YOU for having an interest in either purchasing, stealing, or even opening this book. I appreciate it.

Welcome to my book. Before we start, here are a few housekeeping tips to ensure you have better results, better-tasting food, and lots of fun.

Always set yourself up for success. Mise en place is key. It's the only way to cook efficiently, whether in a professional or home kitchen, so do it! Mise en place means having a clean, well-organized workspace, the right tools at hand (not in the back of the drawer), a stable cutting board (put a damp kitchen towel under it to keep it from moving), a sharp knife, and all your ingredients cleaned, chopped, measured, weighed, and portioned, all ready to go.

Did I mention a sharp knife? This is the most important tool in your arsenal, and it needs to be *sharp*. A sharp knife will make food prep easier, make it safer (dull knives end up not cutting well and causing injuries), and give you a better chance at success. There are a lot of knives out there, and prices can get out of hand. Go for what feels comfortable to handle and a price point that won't make you stressed every time you use it. Invest in a sharpening tool like a steel or sharpening stone to keep it razor-sharp. Always remember to clean the blade after you sharpen it, as the sharpening will leave some metal dust on the blade.

So there you are, looking good, all set up, ready to go. Now put on a favourite playlist and have fun! Here are a few more tips.

Simplicity is key. This is true when it comes to cooking but also when it comes to your cooking tools. Remember, somebody is gonna have to wash all this stuff up after! I love washing dishes, it's my zen space, but not everybody agrees. So keep that in mind when you're cooking. I have one spatula, one whisk, one pastry cutter (don't judge), one fine-mesh strainer, and one bread knife that I use for almost anything but bread. Find what works for you, and keep it simple, and just cook like no one's watching.

You will probably notice right away that my recipes call for salted butter. Yes, you're reading that right. Life's too short, and unsalted butter is a crime. There, I said it.

While we're on the subject, salt is, well . . . salt. There are so many different salts out there these days—cooking salts, fine and coarse salts, all kinds of finishing salts—but ultimately any salt will do. So don't stop yourself from cooking a recipe because you don't have the "right" salt. I use kosher salt and sea salt (my favourite is Newfoundland Salt Company sea salt). And pepper is always freshly cracked. Always.

You might also notice that no recipes call for any type of alcohol, not even a splash of wine for deglazing. I quit drinking sixteen years ago because I was losing control. I had just opened my first restaurant, and the ultimate high of fulfilling my lifelong dream was just too much to handle, and things went downhill. At the time, quitting was not very popular and seemed almost unrealistic given the amount of drinking in the restaurant industry and the trench I had dug myself into. I read my first restaurant review in rehab, thanks to a counsellor who thought a little positive reinforcement would do me good. Needless to say, quitting drinking has changed my life in so many ways it's hard to describe. Now I can focus on my work and my family and enjoy being present in every moment. I consider it my greatest achievement. It has allowed me to do so much that I never thought was even remotely possible. So if any of you out there feel that you are losing your grip, get help. You're worth it!

Now on to my toughest critics . . . Cooking at home is a fairly new career for me, and my kids are six and eight years old, so I would say I have a good eight years under my belt and probably another fifteen before I retire and let the new generation feed me! They love to "cook," by which I mean chop stuff, make a mess, eat most of the mise en place, and complain that they're hungry and that everything takes so long, so yeah, I guess you can say they cook. Away from the hectic pace of cooking on the line, where everything is done at lightning speed with precision and detail in unison with the brigade a hundred times over in an evening, cooking at home is slow, requires a good playlist, and will get done in multiple steps during the day and might require a few stops. I like to start early in the morning, after I drop the kids off at school. Most of my dinner is planned, the mise en place is started, and a list of things I might need starts to take form. Everything comes together between piano lessons, homework, and/or a game of shinny at the park. All that organizing and planning pays off when you get a thumbs-up or a heartfelt "mmmmm." That being said, I do get some bad reviews, but not enough to shut me down! All these recipes have been vetted, reviewed, and starred or pooh-poohed by my two boys. I love you guys and wouldn't want to cook for anybody else! Also, good luck getting anybody else to make you freshly squeezed orange juice and a cheese omelette on a rainy Tuesday morning before school.

The recipes in this book are all on steady rotation in our house, some for weeknight dinners, some for a treat on weekends, and some for special occasions. Some nights are hectic and may result in an early dinner for the boys and leftovers or a late-night cheese plate for Mom and Dad, but for the most part dinner is sacred at our house. Balancing everything is work in itself, but I try to set up my day in a way that I can get dinner ready in the most efficient way possible, all mise en place and prepping veggies in the morning, a little assembly before I pick up the kids from school, and the finishing touches during homework. Voilà—a three-course meal in under 30 minutes, with no more than another 45 minutes of prep during the day. But, sometimes I'm on the road for two weeks at a time and this schedule goes out the window. That's life! Find a rhythm and schedule that works for you.

Living in Montréal has always been a big influence on my cooking, whether it's the four distinct seasons, the multiculturalism that has enriched our food landscape, or good old Québec culinary traditions. The long winters make us appreciate the summer heat, just as fall and spring bring us our local seafood and cabane à sucre. In these pages you'll find some of my favourite family recipes, seasonal classics, and a cabane à sucre feast.

Enjoy these recipes. Hopefully they can inspire you to just have fun and cook. So, let's get prepping!

Breakfast

Biscuit
Breakfast Sandwiches

Makes 6 sandwiches

The essential part of this recipe is the homemade biscuit. Or is it the runny egg yolk? Let's just say it's a tie. Like most iconic fast-food chains, you need a good breakfast sandwich in your back pocket. Making delicious biscuits from scratch is fast and easy. This breakfast combines a lot of things I love: warm buttered biscuits, creamy, runny egg yolk, and a little spice. Say goodbye to the drive-thru!

1 batch Flaky Sour Cream Biscuits (page 35), warm

6 eggs, fried

6 slices smoked ham

6 slices sharp cheddar cheese

Pickled Jalapeños (page 263)

1 Cut the warm biscuits in half horizontally. Place a fried egg on each bottom half. Layer each with a slice of ham, a slice of cheddar, and some pickled jalapeños, then close the sandwiches.

Pancakes with Whipped Butter and Peach Preserves

Serves 4

Pancakes are a real treat at any breakfast. And if you have kids, you need to become a pro at making them, so here's my foolproof recipe. Peach preserves are my favourite. My mom makes them every year with fresh peaches, and as a kid, I would look forward to the new batch every summer. These days I add vanilla and use a little less sugar than my mom did. The preserves are delicious with the pancakes, but I also like to add them to yogurt, spread them on buttered toast, or eat them straight from the jar.

Peach Preserves (Makes 2 cups)

2 pounds (900 g) ripe peaches

½ cup granulated sugar

½ teaspoon kosher salt

1 vanilla bean, split lengthwise and seeds scraped out

Whipped Butter

½ pound (225 g) salted butter, at room temperature

Pancakes

1½ cups whole milk

¼ cup white vinegar

½ vanilla bean, split lengthwise and seeds scraped out

2 large eggs

2 cups all-purpose flour

2 tablespoons granulated sugar

2 tablespoons baking powder

1 tablespoon baking soda

Pinch of kosher salt

4 tablespoons salted butter, melted

1 Make the peach preserves: Fill a large bowl with ice water. Bring a large pot of water to a boil over high heat. Using a small knife, cut a shallow X on the bottom of each peach. This will allow the skin to easily pull away once the peaches are blanched. Working in batches of 3 or 4 peaches at a time, submerge the peaches in the boiling water and blanch for 30 seconds. Using a slotted spoon, remove the peaches from the boiling water and plunge them into the bowl of ice water until cool enough to handle. Empty the pot and set aside.

2 Peel the peaches. (You might need to use a small paring knife to remove all the skin.) Cut the peaches into quarters and discard the pits. Place the peaches in the pot. Mix in the sugar, salt, and vanilla bean seeds. Bring the mixture to a light boil over medium-high heat, then reduce the heat to low and simmer, uncovered and stirring often, until the mixture thickens, about 45 minutes. Remove from the heat and let cool to room temperature before serving. Completely cooled peach preserves can be stored in an airtight container in the fridge for up to 2 weeks. If properly canned, the preserves can be stored in a cool, dry place for up to 1 year.

3 Make the whipped butter: In a medium bowl using a hand-held electric mixer, whip the butter on high speed until light and fluffy and doubled in size. Set aside.

recipe continues

4 Make the pancakes: Preheat the oven to 200°F (100°C). Line a baking sheet with parchment paper.

5 Combine the milk and white vinegar in a large bowl and let sit at room temperature for 15 minutes. Add the vanilla bean seeds and eggs and whisk until combined.

6 In a medium bowl, stir together the flour, sugar, baking powder, baking soda, and salt.

7 Add the dry ingredients to the wet ingredients in 3 additions, stirring after each addition just until no dry bits remain. Do not overmix. Stir in the melted butter.

8 Heat an 11-inch cast-iron crêpe pan or large nonstick frying pan over medium heat. Cook 3 pancakes at a time, ladling about ⅓ cup of batter per pancake into the hot pan. Cook until the edges are golden brown on the bottom and bubbles start to form on the surface, about 90 seconds. Flip the pancakes and cook until golden brown on the other side, about another 90 seconds. Transfer the pancakes to the lined baking sheet and keep warm in the oven while you cook the remaining pancakes.

9 Serve the pancakes with the whipped butter and peach preserves.

Québec Snow Crab Omelette with Wild Ramp Pesto

Serves 1

Omelettes are more than just breakfast. In the cooking world, they're more like a rite of passage: three eggs, salt, and butter. Classic, simple, perfect! Only thing is, being so simple makes it hard to cover up if you don't get it right. (You can also toss three eggs in a pan with butter, mix it up, and get a great result!) Although I like to break a lot of cooking "rules," this method is not one of them. Try it, you'll see. A perfect omelette is not only better tasting but it also gives you the satisfaction of a job well done.

In Québec, the melting snow brings us some of my favourite foods: wild ramps and snow crab. Something about the sweetness of the crab combined with the creaminess of the eggs and the sharp bite of ramp pesto just works.

Wild Ramp Pesto
(Makes about 2 cups)

1 pound (450 g) wild ramps

2 garlic cloves, crushed

½ cup grated Grana Padano cheese

Zest and juice of 1 lemon

Kosher salt

Freshly cracked black pepper

¾ cup olive oil

For 1 omelette

3 large eggs

Kosher salt

2 tablespoons salted butter

1½ ounces (40 g) Québec snow crab meat, picked over for bits of shell

1 Make the wild ramp pesto: Trim the roots of the ramps and roughly chop them.

2 Fill a large bowl with ice water. Fill a large pot with salted water and bring to a boil. Add the ramps and blanch for 45 seconds. Using a slotted spoon, remove the ramps from the boiling water and plunge them into the bowl of ice water. Once cooled, drain the ramps and spread on a plate lined with a kitchen towel to dry.

3 In a blender, combine the ramps, garlic, cheese, lemon zest and juice, and a pinch each of salt and pepper. With the blender running on medium-high speed, slowly stream in the olive oil and blend until smooth. Scrape the pesto into a small bowl or jar and set aside. Leftover ramp pesto can be stored in an airtight container in the fridge for up to 1 month.

4 Make the omelette: In a small bowl, combine the eggs and salt and beat with a fork.

recipe continues

5 Heat a medium nonstick frying pan over medium heat. Once the pan is hot, add the butter and let it melt, tilting the pan to coat the bottom. Reduce the heat to medium-low and pour in the eggs. Using a rubber spatula, mix the eggs constantly in a figure eight motion until the eggs begin to cook and come together. Once the eggs begin to resemble very loose scrambled eggs, use the spatula to make sure they cover the whole bottom of the pan and stop mixing. Then spread the crab meat all over and cook until the eggs look nice and creamy, about 30 seconds. Remove from the heat and, using the spatula, carefully roll the omelette over itself. Gently roll the omelette onto a plate and top it with some wild ramp pesto.

Buckwheat Crêpes with Ham, Asparagus, and Béchamel Sauce Serves 4 to 6

This recipe reminds me of when I was young and my mom and I went to eat crêpes at the Crêperie à la Gourmandise Bretonne, in Saint-Sauveur. This was my favourite crêpe and still is. Now I make these at home for my family on lazy weekends.

1 cup buckwheat flour

¾ cup all-purpose flour

1½ teaspoons kosher salt

1 large egg

1¼ cups whole milk

1 tablespoon salted butter, melted

1⅓ cups water

10 slices smoked ham

1 pound (450 g) asparagus, trimmed, blanched, and cooled

1 batch Béchamel Sauce (page 256)

1 Make the buckwheat crêpes: In a medium bowl, stir together the buckwheat flour, all-purpose flour, and salt.

2 In a separate medium bowl, whisk together the egg, milk, butter, and water.

3 Pour the wet ingredients into the dry ingredients and whisk until smooth.

4 Heat an 11-inch cast-iron crêpe pan over medium-high heat. Ladle about ¼ cup of batter into the middle of the pan. Using a crêpe spatula, spread the batter in a circular motion to cover the entire bottom of the pan. (Alternatively, ladle the batter into the pan and tilt the pan to evenly coat the bottom.) Cook for about 15 seconds, until lightly browned on the bottom. Using the spatula, flip the crêpe and cook the other side for another 15 seconds. Transfer the crêpe to a large plate and cover with a kitchen towel to keep warm and prevent it from drying out while you cook the remaining crêpes. You should have 10 crêpes.

5 Assemble and broil: Position a rack 6 inches under the broiler. Set the oven to broil.

6 Working with one crêpe at a time, place a crêpe on a cutting board with the browner side down. Lay a slice of ham over the crêpe. Lay a few asparagus spears on the ham at the end closest to you and tightly roll up the crêpe. Trim the ends, then cut the rolled crêpe into 4 even pieces. Repeat to fill, roll, and cut the remaining crêpes.

7 Arrange all the rolled crêpe pieces, cut side up, in a 13 × 9-inch baking dish. Pour the béchamel sauce evenly over top. Broil until the sauce is golden brown, about 5 minutes.

Hot Dog Bun French Toast

Serves 4

Nothing beats roasting hot dogs on an open fire in the summer, but in my family most times we don't eat the buns . . . until the next morning! Soft and chewy hot dog buns are the perfect sponge, making them ideal for French toast. Cooked to golden-brown perfection on each side, they become slightly crispy on the outside and super moist in the middle. Hold the mustard on these buns!

3 large eggs

1 cup whole milk

2 tablespoons pure maple syrup

½ teaspoon kosher salt

½ vanilla bean, split lengthwise and seeds scraped out

4 teaspoons salted butter, divided, for frying

4 hot dog buns, split in half

For serving

Fresh berries

Pure maple syrup

1 In a large bowl, whisk together the eggs, milk, maple syrup, salt, and vanilla bean seeds.

2 Melt 2 teaspoons of the butter in a medium nonstick frying pan over medium-low heat. While the butter is melting, place 2 split buns into the egg mixture, turning them over and allowing them to soak. Once the butter is bubbling, remove the buns from the mixture, allowing excess to drip back into the bowl, and place the buns cut side down in the pan. Cook, turning once, for about 2 minutes per side, until golden brown. Add another 2 teaspoons butter to the pan, and soak and cook the remaining buns.

3 Serve the buns with berries and maple syrup.

Savoury Breakfast Bread Pudding

Serves 6 to 8

Savoury bread pudding is a great way to use up leftovers and feed a bunch of hungry kids (and adults). This one-pan dish is perfect for a sleepover breakfast, brunch, or a lazy dinner with some simple greens or a salad.

2 tablespoons vegetable oil

2 medium yellow onions, thinly sliced

10 cups day-old bread torn into pieces

2 cups grated cheddar cheese

1 cup julienned smoked ham

4 large eggs

1⅓ cups + 2 tablespoons milk (any typo)

⅔ cup heavy (35%) cream

1 tablespoon fresh thyme leaves

1 tablespoon kosher salt

1 teaspoon freshly cracked black pepper

2 tablespoons salted butter, cut into small cubes

1 Preheat the oven to 350°F (180°C). Grease a 13 × 9-inch baking dish.

2 Heat the vegetable oil in a large frying pan over medium-low heat. Add the onions and cook, stirring often, until golden brown, 25 to 30 minutes.

3 Scrape the cooked onions into the prepared baking dish. Add the bread, cheddar, and ham and mix together.

4 In a medium bowl, whisk together the eggs, milk, cream, thyme, salt, and pepper. Pour the egg mixture over the bread mixture and gently mix everything together. Let rest for 10 minutes.

5 Cover the dish with foil and bake for 30 minutes. Remove the foil, scatter the cubed butter over the bread pudding, and bake for another 15 to 20 minutes, until the top is golden brown and crispy. Let the bread pudding cool for 5 minutes before serving.

Chocolate Banana Buns

Makes 12 buns

When my partners and I were opening our first restaurant, Garde Manger in Old Montréal, we had no idea what we were doing. The only thing we knew we could do was cook, make drinks, and play some good tunes. Looking back, the fact that we were inexperienced probably helped a lot. Every decision was made on the fly, we had no real plans or money, but we were young and living out our dream of opening a restaurant. Through a month of nonstop construction, we had a lot of snacks to keep us going! Even standing up and holding a two-by-four, we always had coffee and snacks. We would start most mornings with chocolate banana buns from Olive + Gourmando, one of the most iconic café/ bakeries in Old Montréal that for over twenty years has set the standard for service, quality, and taste in our neighbourhood. This is my version of those unforgettable buns—they're decadent, chewy, sweet, and a little salty. Enjoy—but not every morning!

Filling

½ cup salted butter, softened

1 cup granulated sugar

½ cup unsweetened cocoa powder

1 cup finely chopped semisweet dark chocolate

6 ripe bananas, sliced into rounds

Buns

1½ cups whole milk, warm

½ cup granulated sugar

4½ teaspoons instant yeast

2 eggs, at room temperature

2 egg yolks, at room temperature

½ cup salted butter, melted

6 cups all-purpose flour

2 teaspoons kosher salt

Cream Cheese Icing (optional)

8 ounces (225 g) cream cheese, at room temperature

6 tablespoons salted butter, at room temperature

1 teaspoon pure vanilla extract

1½ cups icing sugar

1 Make the filling: In a medium bowl using a hand-held electric mixer, or in a stand mixer fitted with the paddle attachment, cream the butter and granulated sugar. Add the cocoa powder and chocolate. Mix well until combined and smooth.

2 Make the buns: In a large bowl, stir together the warm milk, granulated sugar, and yeast. Add the whole eggs, egg yolks, and melted butter and mix well. Sprinkle in the flour and salt and stir with a wooden spoon until a shaggy dough starts to form. Transfer the dough to a lightly floured work surface. Using your hands, knead the dough for about 10 minutes, until smooth.

recipe continues

3 Place the dough in a well-oiled large bowl, turning it to coat with oil. Cover the bowl with a kitchen towel and let the dough rest on the counter until doubled in size, 1 to 1½ hours.

4 Butter a 13 × 9-inch baking dish. Once the dough has doubled in size, transfer it to a floured work surface and roll it out into a 21 × 14-inch rectangle. Orient the dough with a long side facing you. Spread the filling over the dough, leaving a ¼-inch exposed border at the top edge. Arrange the sliced bananas evenly over the filling, then tightly roll the dough up into a log, pinching the exposed border at the top to seal the log. With the log seam side down, use a sharp knife to cut it into 12 equal pieces.

5 Place the buns cut side up in the prepared baking dish. Cover with a damp kitchen towel and let sit on the counter until almost doubled in size, 30 to 45 minutes.

6 Meanwhile, preheat the oven to 350°F (180°C).

7 Remove the towel and bake the buns until golden brown around the edges, 25 to 30 minutes. Let the buns cool in the baking dish for 10 minutes.

8 Meanwhile, make the cream cheese icing, if using: In a large bowl using a hand-held electric mixer, or in a stand mixer fitted with the paddle attachment, beat the cream cheese, butter, and vanilla on medium-high speed until light and fluffy. Add half the icing sugar and mix on low speed until combined. Add the remaining icing sugar and beat until smooth.

9 Spread the cream cheese icing (if using) over the chocolate banana buns and serve. Store the buns in an airtight container on the counter for up to 2 days.

Breakfast Mishkabibble

Serves 4

Every Jewish deli in Montréal has its own version of this recipe. Some places call it a corned beef hash, others a mishmash. In my family, we call it a mishkabibble! When we can't make it to our favourite spots (Snowdon Deli, Beautys), this is one of our weekend treats at home. It's basically a mash of potatoes, onions, salami, and tossed eggs. It seems like an omelette but it's not—it's a tasty savoury mess!

6 large eggs

1 tablespoon salted butter

2 tablespoons vegetable oil, divided

1 large yellow onion, thinly sliced

2 garlic cloves, smashed and chopped

3 skin-on russet potatoes, cubed

⅔ pound (300 g) all-beef salami, thinly sliced

Freshly cracked black pepper

Flaky sea salt

For serving

Rye bread, toasted and buttered

Ketchup (page 260) or store-bought

1 Crack the eggs into a medium bowl. Pop the yolks and set aside.

2 Melt the butter and 1 tablespoon of the vegetable oil in a medium nonstick frying pan over medium heat. Once the butter has melted, add the onions and garlic and cook, stirring often, for about 10 minutes, until slightly caramelized. Add the potatoes and continue cooking, stirring often, for about 15 minutes, until the potatoes are slightly browned. Scrape the mixture into a large bowl and set aside.

3 Return the pan to medium heat (no need to wipe it). Add the remaining 1 tablespoon vegetable oil and the salami and cook, stirring often, for 4 or 5 minutes, until the salami is crispy. Return the potatoes and onions to the pan and toss everything together. Add the eggs and a few cracks of pepper and, without stirring, cook for about a minute. Using a spatula, fold the mixture into itself a few times, being careful not to overmix. Once the eggs are cooked, divide between plates. Sprinkle with a bit of flaky sea salt. Serve with buttered rye toast and ketchup.

Bread

Brown Butter
Poppy Seed Muffins

Makes 12 muffins

Many muffin recipes omit the sugar, avoid processed foods, and substitute ingredients to make a "healthier muffin." This recipe does the same but somehow is more decadent! These muffins are a favourite at our house and stay moist for a long time (or as long as they last). If you really want to make it over the top, serve the muffins with more brown butter and a little pinch of sea salt.

1½ cups all-purpose flour

1 cup bran flakes

¼ cup poppy seeds

2 teaspoons baking powder

1 teaspoon baking soda

1 teaspoon kosher salt

3 ripe bananas, lightly mashed but still chunky

4 Medjool dates, pitted and roughly chopped

¼ cup pure maple syrup

¼ cup avocado oil

¼ cup Brown Butter (page 255), melted

½ cup milk (any type)

2 eggs

1 Preheat the oven to 350°F (180°C). Line a 12-cup muffin tin with paper liners or grease with nonstick cooking spray.

2 In a large bowl, stir together the flour, bran flakes, poppy seeds, baking powder, baking soda, and salt.

3 In a medium bowl, combine the mashed bananas, dates, maple syrup, avocado oil, brown butter, milk, and eggs; mix well. You want to see some chunks of banana.

4 Add the wet ingredients to the dry ingredients and mix until just combined. Do not overmix.

5 Divide the batter evenly between the muffin cups. Bake for 20 to 25 minutes, until golden brown and a toothpick inserted into the centre of a muffin comes out clean. Remove the muffins from the tin and let cool for 5 minutes before serving. Store the muffins in an airtight container on the counter for up to 4 days.

Charlie's Corn Loaf

Makes 1 loaf or about 36 mini muffins

My son Charlie and I often team up to make this family-favourite loaf together. Literally dump and stir—just a couple of easy steps and you get the perfect sweet and salty loaf. Moist, with the right amount of crumble, it's a perfect side for a chowder or for a summer brunch with a salad. A versatile recipe that can be easily modified by adding cheese or hot peppers. Feel free to bake in mini muffin tins for little bites for 20 to 25 minutes until golden on top and a skewer inserted into the middle of a muffin comes out clean or cook in a cast-iron pan. This loaf is delicious served warm with butter.

1 cup yellow cornmeal

¾ cup all-purpose flour

1½ teaspoons baking powder

½ teaspoon baking soda

1 teaspoon kosher salt

2 eggs, beaten

¼ cup liquid honey

1½ cups buttermilk

6 tablespoons salted butter, melted

1 cup fresh or frozen corn kernels

1 Preheat the oven to 425°F (220°C). Butter a 9 × 5-inch nonstick loaf pan.

2 In a medium bowl, combine the cornmeal, flour, baking powder, baking soda, and salt and mix well.

3 In a separate medium bowl, mix together the eggs, honey, buttermilk, and butter. Fold in the corn kernels. Pour the wet mixture into the dry mixture and gently stir with a wooden spoon until combined.

4 Pour the batter into the prepared pan and smooth the top. Bake for 50 minutes, until golden on top and a paring knife or skewer inserted into the centre comes out clean. Remove from the oven and allow to cool in the pan for 10 minutes, then gently invert to release the loaf. Serve warm.

5 Once cooled completely, the loaf can be wrapped tightly in plastic wrap and stored on the counter for up to 3 days.

Flaky Sour Cream Biscuits

Makes 6 biscuits

Flaky, buttery biscuits are probably the easiest and best way to elevate any meal. They can be served as a side, turned into a sandwich, or served on their own with a touch of butter, some jam, and a pinch of salt. The hardest part is to not make them for every meal!

2½ cups all-purpose flour

3 teaspoons kosher salt

2 teaspoons baking powder

1 teaspoon granulated sugar

1 teaspoon freshly cracked black pepper, plus more for sprinkling

½ teaspoon baking soda

2 tablespoons thinly sliced fresh chives

½ cup cold salted butter, cubed, plus 2 tablespoons salted butter, melted, for brushing

1¼ cups sour cream

Flaky sea salt, for sprinkling

1 Preheat the oven to 425°F (220°C). Line a baking sheet with parchment paper.

2 In a large bowl, whisk together the flour, salt, baking powder, sugar, pepper, baking soda, and chives. Add the cubed butter and toss to completely coat in flour. Use a pastry cutter to cut the butter into the flour until there are lots of flaky, floury bits of butter. Create a well in the centre of the mixture. Pour in the sour cream and use a fork to mix the sour cream into the flour mixture until large, flaky clumps begin to form. Using your hands, fold the mixture into itself a few times until a lumpy dough begins to form.

3 Turn the dough out onto a lightly floured work surface. Using your hands, knead the dough a couple of times. Using floured hands, shape the dough into an 8 × 4-inch rectangle, about 1 inch thick. Orient the dough with a short side facing you.

4 Fold the dough in thirds as if you are folding a letter: Fold the bottom third up to cover the middle third, and then fold down the top third to cover that same section. It doesn't need to be perfect. Again shape the dough into an 8 × 4-inch rectangle and repeat the folding one more time. This helps create flaky layers in the biscuits. Cut the dough in half lengthwise, and then cut each half into 3 equal pieces. You should have 6 biscuits.

recipe continues

5 Transfer the biscuits to the lined baking sheet, leaving about 2 inches between each biscuit. Gently brush the tops of the biscuits with the melted butter. Top each biscuit with a sprinkle of flaky sea salt and a few cracks of black pepper. Bake until the tops are lightly golden brown, 15 to 20 minutes.

6 These biscuits are best served hot out of the oven. If you have leftovers, they can be stored in an airtight container on the counter for up to 1 day. To reheat, place the biscuits on a parchment-lined baking sheet in a preheated 350°F (180°C) oven for 5 to 6 minutes, until warmed through.

Soft Butter Rolls

Makes 15 rolls

Growing up, I spent one month every summer at sleepaway camp. I had the time of my life, canoe-tripping, spending time in the woods, fishing, and just having fun and making lots of friends. Many things were memorable, but mostly I loved the camp food and the whole dining hall experience—Swedish meatballs, taco night, and occasionally we would get warm homemade butter rolls, the best! I love these rolls buttered and served warm with a chowder.

1 cup whole milk, warmed

2¼ teaspoons instant yeast

2 tablespoons granulated sugar, divided

3 cups all-purpose flour, divided, plus more if needed

1 large egg

4 tablespoons butter, at room temperature

1 teaspoon kosher salt

To finish

3 tablespoons butter, melted, plus more for brushing

Flaky sea salt

1 Make the dough and let rest: In a large bowl, whisk together the milk, yeast, and 1 tablespoon of the sugar. Let sit until the yeast begins to foam, 5 to 7 minutes.

2 When the yeast is active, add 1 cup of the flour, the remaining 1 tablespoon sugar, the egg, room temperature butter, and salt. Mix well with a wooden spoon. Sprinkle in the remaining 2 cups flour and mix until a moist dough forms. The dough should be soft and slightly sticky, but you should be able to knead it with floured hands. If the dough is too wet to knead, mix in another 1 tablespoon flour.

3 Turn the dough out onto a lightly floured work surface. Using lightly floured hands, knead the dough for 3 to 4 minutes, until smooth. Place the dough in a lightly oiled large bowl, turning it to coat with oil. Cover the bowl with a kitchen towel and let the dough rest on the counter until doubled in size, 1½ to 2 hours.

4 Shape the rolls and bake: Butter a 13 × 9-inch baking dish or large cast-iron frying pan.

recipe continues

5 Once the dough has doubled in size, punch it down with your hands to remove the air. Turn the dough out onto an unfloured work surface and use a dough scraper or sharp knife to divide it into 15 equal pieces. Shape each piece into a smooth ball by rolling it under the palm of your hand. Arrange the balls of dough in the prepared baking dish. Cover the dish with a kitchen towel and let the dough rest on the counter until doubled in size, about 1 hour.

6 About 15 minutes before the rolls have finished rising, preheat the oven to 350°F (180°C).

7 When the rolls are ready to bake, brush the tops with melted butter and sprinkle with flaky sea salt. Bake until the tops are golden brown, 20 to 25 minutes. Leftover rolls can be stored in an airtight container on the counter for up to 3 days.

Crusty White Bread

Makes 1 loaf

Making artisanal bread is an art that can take years to master, but great-tasting bread is simple, fun to make, and delicious, and doesn't need any special equipment. This is a great recipe to make bakery-quality bread in a couple of simple steps. But, like a lot of simple but great recipes, it requires time. If you plan properly, most of the work will be done while you sleep!

3½ cups all-purpose flour, plus ½ cup more for dusting

2 teaspoons instant yeast

2 teaspoons kosher salt

1¾ cups warm water

1 Make the dough and let rest: In a large bowl, whisk together the flour, yeast, and salt. Pour in the warm water. Using a wooden spoon, mix until a shaggy, wet dough forms. Cover the bowl tightly with plastic wrap and let the dough rest on the counter, until doubled in size, at least 5 to 6 hours or preferably overnight.

2 Cut a large piece of parchment paper to line a Dutch oven. Remove the top rack from the oven and put the Dutch oven, with the lid on, on the middle rack. Preheat the oven to 450°F (230°C) so that the pan heats up along with the oven for at least 30 minutes.

3 Shape the bread and bake: Once the dough has doubled in size, knead it in the bowl about 8 times. This will create an airy bread.

4 Place ½ cup flour in a large bowl. Place the dough in the bowl and turn it to coat with flour. Transfer the dusted dough, seam side down, onto the parchment paper. Reshape the dough into a round as best you can; it doesn't need to be perfect. I like to make one shallow cut (this is called scoring) in the top with a sharp knife or razor blade so the bread can expand.

recipe continues

5 Carefully remove the hot Dutch oven from the oven and place it on the stovetop. Remove the lid. Using the parchment paper, lift the dough and lower both the dough and the paper into the Dutch oven. Cover with the lid and bake for 30 minutes. Remove the lid and continue to bake the bread until deep golden brown and crispy, 15 to 20 minutes. Carefully remove the bread from the Dutch oven and place it on a wire rack to cool for at least 10 minutes before serving.

6 This bread is best eaten on the day of baking but can be wrapped tightly in plastic wrap and stored on the counter for up to 3 days.

Pita Bread

This pita bread is moist, elastic, and full of flavour. It's very different from dry, thin pita. The texture is chewy and spongy because of the olive oil in the dough. Cook them until they have a nice colour, but don't panic—little burnt spots are tasty!

⅔ cup + 2 teaspoons whole milk, at room temperature

⅓ cup + 1 teaspoon water, at room temperature

2 teaspoons active dry yeast

1 teaspoon granulated sugar

2½ cups all-purpose flour

1 teaspoon kosher salt

1 tablespoon chopped fresh oregano

2 tablespoons olive oil, plus more as needed and for frying

1 Make the dough and let rest: In a small bowl, whisk together the milk, water, yeast, and sugar. Let sit until the yeast begins to foam, 5 to 7 minutes.

2 In a large bowl, stir together the flour, salt, and oregano.

3 When the yeast is active, add the olive oil. Pour the yeast mixture into the flour mixture and mix well with a wooden spoon until a rough dough forms. Transfer the dough to a lightly floured work surface and knead with your hands until the dough is smooth, 4 to 5 minutes.

4 Place the dough in a lightly oiled large bowl, turning it to coat with oil. Cover the bowl with a kitchen towel and let the dough rest on the counter until doubled in size, about 1 hour.

5 Shape the pita and cook: Once the dough has doubled in size, punch it down with your hands to remove the air. Turn the dough out onto an unfloured work surface and use a dough scraper or sharp knife to divide it into 8 equal pieces. Shape each piece into a ball by rolling it under the palm of your hand.

6 Heat a large frying pan over medium heat and drizzle with a bit of the olive oil.

recipe continues

7 On a lightly oiled work surface, use a rolling pin to roll out one ball of dough into a 7-inch circle. Immediately place the rolled-out dough in the pan and cook for 45 to 60 seconds per side, flipping when the dough has slightly puffed and has some golden spots on the bottom. Repeat with the remaining dough balls, rolling out and cooking them one at a time, adding more olive oil as needed. (The dough is very sticky and elastic. You can't roll them all out beforehand because they will stick together and lose their shape.) Store in an airtight container on the counter for up to 3 days.

Focaccia

This is my slightly simplified version of focaccia. I cut corners a little bit, but taking a few steps out doesn't mean it isn't just as good, just a touch faster and more realistic to pull off at home. Basically, focaccia is a crusty, moist sponge flavoured with good-quality olive oil, fresh herbs, and flaky sea salt. It's great for sandwiches, for grilling, and for enjoying with spreads.

5 cups all-purpose flour

1 tablespoon kosher salt

2¼ teaspoons instant yeast

3 cups warm water

2 teaspoons liquid honey

¼ cup good-quality olive oil, plus more for drizzling

Flaky sea salt

Leaves from 1 sprig fresh rosemary, roughly chopped

1 Make the dough and let rest: In a large bowl, stir together the flour, salt, and yeast.

2 In a small bowl, stir together the water and honey. Pour the wet ingredients into the dry ingredients and mix with a wooden spoon until a shaggy dough forms with no dry patches. Pour the olive oil over the dough and, using your hands, gently move the dough around to completely coat it with oil. Cover the bowl tightly with plastic wrap and let the dough rest on the counter until doubled in size, about 1 hour.

3 Shape the focaccia and let rest: Generously oil a 13 × 9-inch baking dish.

4 Once the dough has doubled in size, using oiled hands, grab one side of the dough in the bowl, pull it up, and fold it into the centre. Repeat this action 3 more times, turning the bowl slightly before each fold. Turn the dough out into the baking dish. Using your fingers, gently stretch the dough to fit the dish. Press your fingertips firmly into the dough, forming indentations all over. Let the dough rest, uncovered, on the counter until slightly risen, another 30 minutes.

5 Meanwhile, preheat the oven to 425°F (220°C).

6 Bake the focaccia: After the resting period, drizzle a little more olive oil all over the dough. Sprinkle evenly with flaky sea salt and chopped rosemary. Bake until the focaccia has puffed up and is golden brown, 25 to 30 minutes. Leftover focaccia can be stored in an airtight container on the counter for up to 3 days.

Crackers

This is a quick and simple recipe with ingredients you probably have sitting in your pantry next to a nearly empty box of crackers! This is the cracker at its most simple and basic—a functional, crispy vessel for something delicious that's easy to make fresh and can be made a few days early or kept in the freezer until needed. Any flavour works—see a few of my favourite variations on page 50.

2 cups all-purpose flour

½ teaspoon kosher salt

¼ teaspoon garlic powder

¼ teaspoon sweet paprika

½ cup + 1 tablespoon warm water

2 tablespoons olive oil

1 tablespoon pure maple syrup

1 Arrange the oven racks in the upper and lower thirds of the oven and preheat to 400°F (200°C). Line 2 baking sheets with parchment paper.

2 In a medium bowl, stir together the flour, salt, garlic powder, and paprika.

3 In a small bowl, stir together the water, olive oil, and maple syrup.

4 Pour the wet ingredients into the dry ingredients and mix well with a wooden spoon until a shaggy dough forms. Using your hands, knead the dough a few times until it forms a ball. Cover with a damp kitchen towel and let the dough rest for 10 minutes.

5 On a lightly floured work surface, use a rolling pin to roll out the dough to about ⅛ inch thick. (Alternatively, pass the dough through a pasta machine: On a lightly floured work surface, cut the dough into 4 equal pieces using a knife, then roll out a piece of dough with a rolling pin into a strip about ¼ inch thick. Lightly flour the dough. Set your pasta machine to the widest setting and feed the dough through the machine. Adjust the setting to the next size down and pass the dough through the machine again. Repeat until the dough is about ⅛ inch thick.)

6 Cut the dough into 1½ to 2 inches-wide, even-sized shapes and arrange them on the lined baking sheets, evenly spaced. Bake until lightly browned around the edges, 7 to 9 minutes, rotating the pans halfway through. Store the crackers in an airtight container on the counter for up to 5 days.

Variations

Za'atar Crackers: Add 1 tablespoon of za'atar spice to the dry ingredients.

Spicy Cheese Crackers: Add 1 teaspoon of red chili flakes and ½ cup of grated pecorino cheese (or any hard cheese) to the dry ingredients.

Lemon Dill Crackers: Add the zest of 2 lemons and 1 teaspoon of dried dill to the dry ingredients.

Bagels

Living in Montréal, I'm exactly 900 metres from the best bagel shops in the world. Sorry, NYC, you can have everything else but not the bagels. The best way to eat a bagel is right out of the bag before you even set foot outside the store! That first bite will never be matched—the second you leave the bakery, it's all downhill. You get home, eat a couple more, and freeze the rest, never getting that first bite back. With these bagels, though, you can always have the perfect bite, as close as you'll come to the originals, soft and chewy with a touch of sweetness.

1½ cups warm water

4½ teaspoons instant yeast

1 tablespoon granulated sugar

2 teaspoons kosher salt

1 large egg

1 egg yolk

¼ cup vegetable oil

1 cup liquid honey, divided

5 cups bread flour, plus more if needed

Toppings

Flaky sea salt

Everything bagel spice

Poppy seeds

Sesame seeds

1 Make the dough and let rest: In a large bowl, mix together the water, yeast, sugar, and salt. Add the whole egg, egg yolk, vegetable oil, and ½ cup of the honey; mix well. Sprinkle in the bread flour and mix with a wooden spoon until the dough comes together to form a rough ball. Transfer the dough to a lightly floured work surface and knead for about 5 minutes, until a smooth dough forms, sprinkling in a bit more flour if the dough feels too sticky.

2 Place the dough smooth side up in a lightly oiled large bowl. Cover with a damp kitchen towel and let the dough rest for 20 minutes.

3 Shape the bagels, boil, and bake: Line 2 baking sheets with parchment paper and set aside. Pour 12 cups of water and the remaining ½ cup honey into a large pot and bring to a boil. Cover with a lid and reduce the heat to a simmer while preparing the bagels.

4 Punch down the dough with your hands to remove the air. Turn the dough out onto an unfloured work surface. Use a knife to divide the dough into 12 equal portions.

recipe continues

5 Working with one portion of dough at a time, roll the dough into a rope about 6 inches long. Fold the ends over each other and press down and roll to seal the ends well to ensure the bagels do not come apart while being boiled. Place on the first lined baking sheet. Cover the bagels with a thin kitchen towel and let rest for 20 minutes.

6 Meanwhile, preheat the oven to 450°F (230°C). When the resting time is nearly over, bring the water back to a boil and remove the lid.

7 Working with 3 bagels at a time, gently drop the bagels into the boiling water. As they rise to the surface, turn them over and boil them for another minute. Using a spider strainer, remove the bagels from the water and place them on the same lined baking sheet. Sprinkle the bagels with your choice of toppings. Boil and season the remaining bagels.

8 Arrange the boiled and seasoned bagels, evenly spaced, on the second lined baking sheet. Bake until golden brown, 20 to 25 minutes. Transfer the bagels to a wire rack to cool slightly. The bagels are best eaten right away. Store leftover bagels, sliced in half, in an airtight plastic bag in the freezer for up to 1 month. Reheat the bagel halves in the toaster.

Bagel Garnishes

Smoked Fish Spread

Serves 10 to 12

La Florida! Winters are cold in Montréal, and like a lot of Québecers my grandparents escaped to Florida every winter, and occasionally we would go for a visit. Besides the beach, skateboarding on nice streets, and stone crabs, eating this dip is one of my best memories of those trips. When we're lucky enough to go now, we make sure Grandma stocks up on it before we get there.

8 ounces (225 g) smoked whitefish (such as sturgeon, haddock, or pickerel)

½ cup mayonnaise

½ cup cream cheese, at room temperature

Zest and juice of 1 lemon

1 tablespoon chopped drained capers

1 tablespoon finely chopped shallots

1 tablespoon chopped fresh dill

1 teaspoon chopped fresh flat-leaf parsley

½ teaspoon kosher salt

¼ teaspoon white pepper

1 In a food processor, blitz the smoked fish until it is mostly smooth. Scrape the fish into a large bowl. Add the mayonnaise, cream cheese, lemon zest and juice, capers, shallots, dill, parsley, salt, and white pepper. Mix until fully combined. Leftover fish spread can be stored in an airtight container in the fridge for up to 4 days.

Salmon Gravlax

Smoked salmon on bagels needs no introduction. Store-bought salmon or even smoked salmon spread is a great option. But to bring brunch up a notch, this gravlax is always the star. It's cured, not smoked, giving it a more delicate and tender texture. It looks great too. It's also great on crackers or a salad.

1 pound (450 g) purple beets, grated on the large holes of a box grater

1½ cups kosher salt

1 cup packed brown sugar

1 tablespoon dill seeds

1 tablespoon fennel seeds

1 tablespoon freshly cracked black pepper

1 (2.2-pound/1 kg) fresh skin-on salmon fillet

1 In a large bowl, mix together the beets, salt, brown sugar, dill seeds, fennel seeds, and pepper.

2 Spread half the curing mix evenly in a baking dish that will fit the salmon fillet. Place the salmon flesh side down on the curing mix and gently press down. Sprinkle the remaining curing mix over the salmon to completely cover it. Cover the dish with plastic wrap. Place the salmon in the fridge to cure for at least 24 hours but no more than 48. Every 8 hours, drain any liquid that has accumulated, flip the salmon over, and spread the curing mix so the fillet is completely covered.

3 Once the salmon feels firm to the touch, rinse off the curing mix and pat dry the salmon. Thinly slice the salmon and serve. The salmon can be tightly wrapped in plastic wrap and stored in the fridge for up to 2 weeks.

Chopped Liver Mousse

Serves 10 to 12

Don't cringe just because it's liver! This mousse is a rich and creamy bagel topping. The first time I met my girlfriend Sabrina was at my restaurant. She asked me what I was doing after work, and I told her that I was going to go and eat a chopped liver sandwich at the Main Deli on St-Laurent Boulevard. She replied, "I love chopped liver!" Enough said. This is her family's recipe, and it's become my ultimate favourite.

4 tablespoons olive oil, divided,

4 medium yellow onions, thinly sliced

1½ pounds (675 g) chicken livers, trimmed, rinsed, and patted dry

2 small carrots, peeled and boiled

4 hard-boiled eggs, divided

Pinch of ground nutmeg

½ teaspoon kosher salt, plus more for seasoning

Freshly cracked black pepper

Bread, toasts, or crackers, for serving

1 Heat 2 tablespoons of the olive oil in a large frying pan over medium heat. Add the onions and cook, stirring often, until caramelized, about 30 minutes. Scoop out half of the onions and transfer to a plate; set aside. Add the remaining 2 tablespoons olive oil to the pan, reduce the heat to medium-low, and continue cooking the onions until deeply caramelized and crispy. Drain the oil off the onions. Spread the crispy onions on paper towel to absorb excess oil and season with a bit of salt and pepper. Set aside for garnish.

2 Bring a small pot of salted water to a simmer over low heat. Drop the chicken livers into the simmering water and poach for 5 minutes. Drain the chicken livers and spread them on paper towel to dry.

3 In a food processor, combine the poached chicken livers, boiled carrots, 2 of the hard-boiled eggs, and the reserved caramelized onions. Purée until smooth. Add the nutmeg, salt, and a few cracks of pepper, and stir to combine.

4 Pack the chopped liver into a serving dish and smooth the top. Cover tightly with plastic wrap and refrigerate for at least 2 hours.

5 Just before serving, garnish the mousse with the crispy onions. Thinly slice the remaining 2 hard-boiled eggs and serve over top or on the side. Serve with bread, toasts, or crackers. Cover leftover mousse tightly with plastic wrap and store in the fridge for up to 2 days.

Soups and Stews

Roasted Carrot Soup with Yogurt and Poppy Seeds

Serves 4

In the colder months, my kids like to have soup a couple of times a week. I make small batches, use up what's in the fridge, and switch things up to keep it interesting. Usually you can make a great-tasting soup in under an hour. Sweet, tangy, with a little kick from the ginger, this soup is on regular rotation, and it's become a favourite. It is the best way to use up aging carrots—or my archenemy, baby-cut carrots!

3 pounds (1.35 kg) carrots, peeled and cut into 1-inch chunks

4 tablespoons olive oil, divided

2 teaspoons kosher salt, divided

Freshly cracked black pepper

1 medium yellow onion, roughly chopped

2 garlic cloves, smashed and chopped

1 teaspoon chopped peeled fresh ginger

Zest of ½ orange

8 cups water

3 tablespoons salted butter

¼ cup plain full-fat Greek yogurt

2 teaspoons poppy seeds

1 Preheat the oven to 400°F (200°C). Line a baking sheet with parchment paper.

2 Place the carrots in a large bowl. Drizzle in 3 tablespoons of the olive oil and season the carrots with 1 teaspoon of the salt and a few cracks of black pepper. Toss to coat. Spread the carrots evenly on the lined baking sheet. Roast until soft and slightly caramelized, 30 to 35 minutes.

3 When the carrots are almost done roasting, heat the remaining 1 tablespoon olive oil in a large pot over medium-high heat. Once the oil is hot, add the onions and cook, stirring constantly, until soft and translucent, 3 to 4 minutes. Add the garlic, ginger, and orange zest and continue cooking for another minute. Add the roasted carrots, water, and the remaining 1 teaspoon salt. Bring to a boil, scraping up any browned bits from the bottom of the pot. Reduce the heat, cover with a lid, and simmer for 15 to 20 minutes, until the carrots are tender. Remove from the heat and let cool for 10 to 15 minutes.

4 Working in batches, transfer the soup to a high-speed blender. Add the butter and purée until smooth. Adjust the seasoning as needed. Reheat if needed.

5 Ladle the soup into bowls and top with a spoonful of yogurt and a sprinkle of poppy seeds. Store leftover soup, without toppings, in an airtight container in the fridge for up to 4 days or in the freezer for up to 2 months.

Root Vegetable and Bean Soup

Serves 12

Before having kids, I would always take good vegetables from my mom's garden—perfect peppers, cukes, and tomatoes. But when I started making purées and soups for my two sons, appearance didn't matter, and I started to use all the "ugly" garden leftovers my mom gave me at the end of summer: twisted parsnips, stubby carrots, and even turned-up turnips! Every year, I take those vegetables and turn them into great-tasting hearty soups the whole family loves.

2 tablespoons olive oil

1 medium yellow onion, diced

3 stalks celery, diced

2 carrots, peeled and diced

2 turnips, peeled and diced

2 parsnips, peeled and diced

3 garlic cloves, smashed and chopped

1 can (19 ounces/540 mL) kidney beans, rinsed and drained

1 can (19 ounces/540 mL) Romano beans, rinsed and drained

2 cans (28 ounces/796 mL each) peeled whole tomatoes, crushed with your hands

1 jar (12.7 ounces/375 mL) bomba calabrese or your favourite hot pepper spread

12 cups water

1 tablespoon herbes de Provence

4 bay leaves

1½ tablespoons kosher salt

1 teaspoon freshly cracked black pepper

1 Heat the olive oil in a large pot over medium-high heat. Once the oil is hot, add the onions, celery, carrots, turnips, and parsnips and cook, stirring often, until the vegetables have slightly softened, 6 to 8 minutes. Add the garlic and cook for another minute.

2 Add the kidney beans, Romano beans, tomatoes and their juice, bomba calabrese, water, herbes de Provence, bay leaves, salt, and pepper. Increase the heat to high and bring to a boil, then reduce the heat to a simmer, cover with a lid, and simmer for 20 to 30 minutes, stirring every so often, until the vegetables are fork-tender. Discard the bay leaves.

3 Ladle the soup into bowls and serve. Store leftover soup in an airtight container in the fridge for up to 4 days or in the freezer for up to 1 month.

Cream of Tomato Soup

Serves 4

This is a fast and easy twist on a classic. Made with canned tomatoes, it still has a fresh, natural taste. Creamy and velvety, with a touch of acidity and not too sweet, it's the perfect bite. My kids ask for this soup all the time!

1 can (28 ounces/796 mL) diced tomatoes

2 garlic cloves, minced

1½ cups water

½ cup heavy (35%) cream

1 teaspoon kosher salt

½ teaspoon freshly cracked black pepper

Crackers (page 49), Spicy Cheese version, for serving

1 In a medium saucepan, combine the tomatoes, garlic, water, cream, salt, and pepper, give it a stir, and bring to a boil. Reduce the heat and simmer, uncovered, for 20 minutes, stirring every few minutes. Once the tomatoes are very tender, purée the soup with an immersion blender. Pass the soup through a fine-mesh strainer into another pot to make sure it's silky smooth.

2 Ladle the soup into bowls and serve with spicy cheese crackers. Store leftover soup in an airtight container in the fridge for up to 4 days or in the freezer for up to 2 months.

Green Borscht

I can't take credit for this recipe. This is my absolute favourite recipe from my mother-in-law. It's a unique chilled summer soup with vibrant flavours and such freshness that it's a must a few times every summer.

1 teaspoon olive oil

½ cup grated peeled carrot

½ cup grated peeled parsnip

1 small yellow onion, diced

1 tablespoon kosher salt

3 large garlic cloves, smashed and chopped

8 cups water

½ cup thinly sliced green onions

1 teaspoon freshly cracked black pepper

4 cups chopped fresh spinach

¼ cup chopped fresh dill, plus 4 sprigs for garnish

Garnishes

4 hard-boiled eggs, quartered

4 tablespoons full-fat sour cream

1 Heat the olive oil in a large pot over medium heat. Once the oil is hot, drop in the carrots, parsnip, onions, and salt and cook, stirring often, until the vegetables are soft and the onions are translucent, about 10 minutes.

2 Add the garlic and cook for another minute.

3 Pour in the water and add the green onions and pepper. Bring to a boil, then reduce the heat to low and simmer, uncovered, for 10 minutes. Stir in the spinach and the dill, then remove the soup from the heat and let cool to room temperature.

4 To serve, ladle the soup into bowls. Top each with a quartered hard-boiled egg, a spoonful of sour cream, and a sprig of fresh dill. Leftover soup, without toppings, can be stored in an airtight container in the fridge for up to 4 days.

Corn Chowder

When in season, corn on the cob is hard to beat with a touch of butter and a pinch of salt. But it's usually so good it doesn't need anything. I like to eat mine plain, all natural, just like that! I never get tired of it, but my family does. So, to switch it up, I like to make chowder that uses every bit of the corn to get the most flavour when it's at its peak.

Corn Stock

6 sweet corn cobs, shucked

1 tablespoon olive oil

2 shallots, thinly sliced

1 stalk celery, roughly chopped

2 garlic cloves, smashed

8 cups water

2 bay leaves

1 teaspoon whole black peppercorns

1 teaspoon kosher salt

Corn Chowder

3 tablespoons salted butter

1 large yellow onion, diced

1 cup diced peeled carrots

1 cup diced celery

2 garlic cloves, smashed and chopped

1½ cups diced peeled Yukon Gold potatoes

5½ cups fresh sweet corn kernels (reserved from corn stock)

Corn stock (at left)

1½ cups whole milk

1½ cups heavy (35%) cream

3 teaspoons kosher salt

1½ teaspoons freshly cracked black pepper

1 cup thinly sliced green onions, for garnish

1 Make the corn stock: Using a serrated knife, slice the kernels off the corn cobs and set aside for the chowder. Set aside the cobs.

2 Heat the olive oil in a medium pot over medium-high heat. Once the oil is hot, add the shallots and cook, stirring, for about a minute. Add the celery and garlic and cook for another minute. Add the stripped corn cobs, water, bay leaves, peppercorns, and salt and bring to a boil, then reduce the heat to low, cover tightly with a lid, and simmer for 45 to 60 minutes, stirring every so often, until the water has taken on a light yellow colour. While the stock is simmering, prepare the ingredients for the chowder. Once the stock is done, strain it through a fine-mesh strainer into a large bowl. Discard or compost the solids.

recipe continues

3 Make the chowder: Melt the butter in a large soup pot over medium heat. Once the butter is melted and foaming, add the onions and cook, stirring often, for 2 to 4 minutes, until soft and translucent. Add the carrots, celery, and garlic and cook, stirring often, for another 1 to 2 minutes, until the carrots are bright orange and the celery is slightly softened. Add the potatoes, corn kernels, and corn stock; bring to a boil. Once it reaches a boil, add the milk, cream, salt, and pepper, stir, and bring just to a simmer. Do not boil. Reduce the heat to maintain a simmer and cook, uncovered, for 30 to 40 minutes, until the potatoes are soft. Taste and adjust the seasoning.

4 To serve, ladle the soup into bowls and sprinkle with the green onions. Store leftover soup in an airtight container in the fridge for up to 4 days or in the freezer for up to 2 months.

Matzoh Ball Soup with Chicken Meatballs

Serves 4

Montréal is a melting pot of diverse cultures, and this is reflected in our food. People from different backgrounds from all over the world have made this one of the best food cities in the world. Many Eastern European immigrants have left their mark on the city with some of our most celebrated foods, like bagels and smoked meat.

When I was a kid, after hockey practice we would eat at Snowdon Deli. It's a classic, with a rich history, and it hasn't changed much since 1946. My favourite was matzoh ball soup, and it still is. This is my mashup version with chicken meatballs that my kids love.

Chicken Meatballs (Makes 12 meatballs)

1 pound (450 g) ground chicken

1 large egg

⅓ cup matzoh meal

2 garlic cloves, minced

1 tablespoon chopped fresh flat-leaf parsley

1 tablespoon chopped fresh dill

2 teaspoons kosher salt

1 teaspoon freshly cracked black pepper

1 tablespoon vegetable oil, for searing

Matzoh Balls (Makes 8 matzoh balls)

2 large eggs

¼ cup vegetable oil or schmaltz

3 tablespoons water or chicken stock

¾ teaspoon kosher salt

½ teaspoon freshly cracked black pepper

1 egg white

¾ cup matzoh meal

Broth

8 cups Chicken Stock (page 264) or store-bought

1 cup chopped peeled carrots

3 tablespoons chopped fresh dill, plus more for garnish

1 Make the chicken meatballs: Place the ground chicken in a large bowl. Add the egg, matzoh meal, garlic, parsley, dill, salt, and pepper. Using wet hands, mix well. Divide the mixture into 12 equal portions and shape into balls. Place the balls on a plate, cover loosely with plastic wrap, and transfer to the fridge to chill while you make the matzoh ball dough.

recipe continues

2 Make the matzoh ball dough: In a large bowl, mix together the eggs, vegetable oil, water, salt, and pepper.

3 In a small bowl, beat the egg white to stiff peaks.

4 Sprinkle the matzoh meal all over the egg and oil mixture. Add the beaten egg white and gently fold together with a spatula. Cover the bowl with plastic wrap and refrigerate for 20 minutes to allow the dough to rest.

5 While the dough is resting, bring a large pot of salted water to a boil, sear the chicken meatballs, and prepare the broth.

6 Sear the chicken meatballs: Heat the vegetable oil in a large pot over medium-high heat. Once the oil is hot, working in batches so you don't crowd the pot, sear the chicken meatballs, turning, until golden brown all over. Transfer to a plate.

7 Make the broth: Once all the meatballs are seared, return them to the pot and pour in the chicken stock. Bring to a boil, then reduce the heat to low, cover with a lid, and simmer the meatballs while you roll and cook the matzoh balls.

8 Roll and cook the matzoh balls: After the resting period, divide the matzoh dough into 8 equal portions and gently roll them into balls, being careful not to squeeze them too tight. Carefully drop the matzoh balls into the boiling water, then reduce the heat to medium-low, cover with a lid, and simmer for 50 to 60 minutes, until cooked through. To test doneness, remove a ball from the pot and cut it in half. It should be uniform in colour and texture.

9 At the 50-minute mark, add the carrots to the broth, cover, and simmer with the chicken meatballs for 10 minutes. When the matzoh balls are done, stir the dill into the broth.

10 When ready to serve, using a slotted spoon, place 2 matzoh balls and 3 meatballs in each bowl. Add a big ladle of broth with a few pieces of carrot and garnish with more dill. Store the soup, without the dill garnish, in an airtight container in the fridge for up to 1 day. Left in the fridge overnight, the matzoh balls get slightly firmer but are still soft and fluffy.

Seafood Chowder

Serves 4 to 6

My love of seafood is one of the reasons I got into cooking. A lifetime ago, my mom was a flight attendant for Quebecair, an airline that serviced Québec's Gaspésie and Côte-Nord regions, where most of our local seafood comes from. She would come home with whelks, shrimp, crab, and lobster, and we would sit with my grandmother and dig in like a pack of sea lions! I've loved to cook and eat seafood ever since, and this chowder is one of our favourites today. It can be made with any seafood or leftover fish, and topping the thick, creamy chowder with homemade croutons makes this dish hard to beat.

4 slices thick-cut bacon, diced

½ cup water

3 tablespoons salted butter

1 medium yellow onion, diced

1 leek (white and light green parts only), halved lengthwise and thinly sliced crosswise

3 stalks celery, diced

3 garlic cloves, minced

3 tablespoons all-purpose flour

4 cups Fish Stock (page 265) or store-bought

1 cup whole milk

1 cup table (18%) cream

1 can (10 ounces/284 g) whole shelled baby clams, drained and juice reserved

2 medium russet potatoes, peeled and cut into 1-inch cubes

11 ounces (300 g) haddock, cut into 2-inch cubes

7 ounces (200 g) cooked snow crab meat, picked over for bits of shell

1 teaspoon kosher salt

½ teaspoon freshly cracked black pepper

3 tablespoons chopped fresh flat-leaf parsley

1 batch Croutons (page 149), for garnish

1 Combine the bacon and water in a large pot and bring to a boil over high heat, stirring often. Once the water has completely evaporated, reduce the heat to medium and continue cooking the bacon until golden brown, 5 to 8 minutes. Scoop out the bacon, leaving the fat in the pot, and set aside.

2 Add the butter, onions, leeks, and celery to the pot and cook for 3 to 4 minutes, stirring often, until the vegetables are soft and translucent. Add the garlic and cook for another minute. Sprinkle in the flour and cook for 2 minutes, stirring constantly. Stir in the fish stock, milk, cream, and reserved clam juice, then increase the heat to high and bring to a boil, stirring often. Once boiling, reduce the heat to low, toss in the potatoes, and simmer, uncovered, for 15 minutes. Add the clams, reserved bacon, haddock, crab meat, salt, and pepper and simmer for another 5 minutes. Taste and adjust the seasoning.

3 Stir in the parsley and ladle the chowder into bowls. Top with the croutons. Store leftover soup, without croutons, in an airtight container in the fridge for up to 4 days.

Sausage, Lentil, and Kale Soup

Serves 4 to 6

I like to keep dried chorizo in the fridge so I can make this soup whenever the urge strikes. Chorizo adds a great smoked paprika flavour and a little bit of tasty fat that adds a lot of depth and richness while keeping the soup light but still really comforting. It's great as a starter or served with some bread and butter alongside a simple salad as a meal.

1 teaspoon olive oil, plus more for drizzling

2 dried chorizo sausages (about 11 ounces/300 g total), sliced into ¼-inch rounds

1 medium yellow onion, diced

2 carrots, peeled and sliced into thin rounds

2 stalks celery, diced

2 garlic cloves, smashed and chopped

½ teaspoon kosher salt

1 tablespoon Italian seasoning

2 tablespoons tomato paste

8 cups Chicken Stock (page 264) or store-bought

2 cups water

1 cup dried green lentils, rinsed and drained

2 cups chopped curly kale

1 Heat the olive oil in a large pot over medium-high heat. Once the oil is hot, add the sausage and sear, stirring often, until slightly coloured all over, about 2 minutes. Add the onions, carrots, celery, and garlic and cook, stirring occasionally, for 4 to 5 minutes, until the vegetables are soft and the onions are translucent and beginning to brown. Reduce the heat to medium, stir in the salt, Italian seasoning, and tomato paste, and cook for another 2 minutes.

2 Pour in the chicken stock and the water and bring to a boil. Once boiling, add the lentils, then reduce the heat to a simmer, cover tightly with a lid, and cook until the lentils have softened, 20 to 25 minutes. Stir in the kale, cover, and simmer for another 5 minutes.

3 Ladle the soup into bowls and drizzle with a bit of olive oil. Store leftover soup in an airtight container in the fridge for up to 4 days or in the freezer for up to 2 months.

Vegetables

Chopped Egg, Radish, and Cucumber Salad with Ranch Dressing

Serves 4

This is one of my favourite summer salads. Crunchy, creamy, and full of fresh herbs with some bite from the radish. It's refreshing and rich all at the same time.

Home-Style Ranch Dressing

½ cup sour cream

¼ cup mayonnaise

¼ cup Homemade Buttermilk (page 254) or store-bought

1 small garlic clove, minced

½ tablespoon onion powder

½ tablespoon chopped fresh flat-leaf parsley

½ tablespoon chopped fresh chives

½ tablespoon chopped fresh dill

½ teaspoon kosher salt

½ teaspoon freshly cracked black pepper

Salad

6 hard-boiled eggs, quartered

8 radishes, halved or quartered (depending on size)

2 cups chopped English cucumber

1 Make the home-style ranch dressing: In a large bowl, combine the sour cream, mayonnaise, buttermilk, garlic, onion powder, parsley, chives, dill, salt, and pepper. Whisk until fully combined. Set aside until ready to use or store in an airtight container in the fridge for up to 5 days.

2 Assemble the salad: In a medium bowl, combine the eggs, radishes, and cucumbers. Stir in a few tablespoons of the ranch dressing to combine. Serve immediately.

Cauliflower Salad with Lemon and Black Pepper Dressing

Serves 4 to 6

This late-fall, early-winter salad came together while I was staring into my fridge with absolutely no idea what to make for dinner. It's the perfect mix of crunchy, creamy, and sweet, with a rich dressing and bitter endive to keep it light. Using up odds and ends to make something tasty is always a plus. Serve this as a side for pork or lamb, or even as a quick lunch on its own.

Lemon and Black Pepper Dressing

½ cup mayonnaise

½ cup plain full-fat Greek yogurt

Zest of 2 lemons

¼ cup freshly squeezed lemon juice

¼ cup cold water

2 garlic cloves, minced

½ teaspoon kosher salt

Freshly cracked black pepper

Cauliflower Salad

1 head cauliflower, leaves removed, quartered

1 head red endive

1 tablespoon olive oil

1 teaspoon flaky sea salt

Freshly cracked black pepper

2 ripe Bartlett pears

1 cup chopped toasted walnuts

1 Make the lemon and black pepper dressing: In a medium bowl, combine the mayonnaise, yogurt, lemon zest, lemon juice, cold water, garlic, kosher salt, and pepper. Whisk until smooth. Set aside until ready to use or store in an airtight container in the fridge for up to 4 days.

2 Make the cauliflower salad: Using a mandoline, carefully slice the cauliflower lengthwise about ⅛ inch thick. Place it in a large bowl.

3 Trim away the root end of the endive and separate the leaves. When no more leaves come off, cut a bit more off the bottom and continue until all the leaves are separated. Add the leaves to the bowl with the cauliflower. Add the olive oil, flaky sea salt, and pepper and toss together. Arrange on a platter.

4 Working with one pear at a time, place a pear on a cutting board and use a paring knife to cut it in half lengthwise. Cut each half in half again lengthwise to create quarters. Cut out the core. Using a mandoline, thinly slice the pears lengthwise. Arrange the pear slices over the cauliflower and endive. Sprinkle with the toasted walnuts and drizzle the lemon and black pepper dressing over the salad. Serve immediately.

Brussels Sprouts with Spicy Maple Vinaigrette

Serves 4

This is Christopher Merrick's famous brussels sprout recipe he put on the menu at Garde Manger when he became the head chef. It quickly became a fall classic at the restaurant, and at my house too. The warm, sweet, spicy vinaigrette sticks to the brussels sprouts and, according to my kids, makes them highly edible!

Spicy Maple Vinaigrette

3 tablespoons olive oil

1 cup thinly sliced shallots

4 garlic cloves, smashed and chopped

½ cup bomba calabrese or your favourite hot pepper spread

½ cup pure maple syrup

1 teaspoon kosher salt

1 teaspoon freshly cracked black pepper

Brussels Sprouts

2 pounds (900 g) brussels sprouts, trimmed and cut in half

2 tablespoons olive oil

2 teaspoons kosher salt

1 teaspoon freshly cracked black pepper

½ cup chopped toasted hazelnuts

1 Make the spicy maple vinaigrette: Heat the olive oil in a large frying pan over medium-high heat. Once the oil is hot, add the shallots and cook for 1 minute. Add the garlic and cook for another minute, stirring frequently. Add the bomba calabrese, maple syrup, salt, and pepper. Bring to a boil and cook, stirring constantly, until the vinaigrette thickens, 1 to 2 minutes. Remove from the heat and set aside.

2 Prepare the brussels sprouts: Preheat the oven to 425°F (220°C). Line a baking sheet with parchment paper.

3 In a large bowl, combine the brussels sprouts, olive oil, salt, and pepper and toss to coat. Spread the brussels sprouts on the lined baking sheet, being careful not to crowd the pan. (Use a second baking sheet if needed.) Roast for 20 to 25 minutes, until the brussels sprouts have caramelized and some of the leaf tips have started to char.

4 Scrape the roasted brussels sprouts into the frying pan with the vinaigrette. Cook over high heat, stirring a few times, until the vinaigrette is sticky and coats the brussels sprouts, about 5 minutes. Toss in the toasted hazelnuts, then transfer to a bowl and serve warm.

Sautéed Greens with Chilies and Fried Garlic

Serves 2 to 4

My favourite Chinese restaurant in Montréal is Mon Nan. I crave their dishes! Sometimes I get takeout, and sometimes I have to go there in person since their salt and pepper squid doesn't travel well. Out of all their dishes, this is the only one I make at home. As a side or to top off some fried rice, it's amazing.

Fried Garlic

1½ cups vegetable oil

3 heads of garlic, cloves separated, peeled, and roughly chopped

¼ teaspoon kosher salt

Sautéed Greens

1 tablespoon garlic oil (reserved from the fried garlic)

4 fresh red chilies, thinly sliced crosswise

4 pounds (1.8 kg) pea greens

½ teaspoon kosher salt

1 teaspoon freshly cracked black pepper

1 Make the fried garlic: Line a baking sheet with paper towel. Place a fine-mesh strainer over a medium metal bowl. Set aside.

2 In a medium saucepan over medium-high heat, heat the vegetable oil with the garlic. Cook, stirring often, for 4 to 5 minutes, until the oil is hot and the garlic is bubbling. Continue cooking for another 4 to 5 minutes, stirring constantly and scraping the sides and bottom of the pot to ensure that the garlic does not stick. As soon as the garlic turns golden brown, carefully strain (the oil is very hot) through the fine-mesh strainer into the metal bowl. Spread the fried garlic on the lined baking sheet and season with salt. Reserve 1 tablespoon of the garlic oil. (Once the oil is cooled, store in an airtight container in the fridge for up to 3 weeks. It's great to use for salad dressings or to cook with.)

3 Sauté the greens: Heat the reserved garlic oil in a large frying pan over medium-high heat. Once the oil is hot, add the chilies and cook, stirring, for about 1 minute. Add the pea greens, salt, and pepper, cover with a lid, and cook until the greens release some of their water, about 1 minute. Remove the lid and sauté for another minute.

4 Transfer the sautéed greens to a serving dish and sprinkle with the fried garlic.

Fried Zucchini Flowers with Gribiche Sauce

Serves 4

This is a special treat. Zucchini flowers are available only for a short period in early summer depending on your climate, so don't miss them. Not stuffing the flowers keeps them crispy and easy to fry, it looks nice, and they deliver pure zucchini flavour. The gribiche sauce with the briny flavour of capers combined with the pickles is a perfect match for the crispy fried flowers. You can skip the gribiche sauce if you want; the fried flowers are also good on their own, served like chips with some hot sauce for dipping.

You can use either male or female flowers; I like to take out the pistils and stamens, but both are edible and can be left in. The female flower has small zucchini attached on the bottom and the male doesn't, but both are equally tasty.

Gribiche Sauce

2 tablespoons grainy Dijon mustard

2 tablespoons white balsamic vinegar

5 tablespoons olive oil

2 tablespoons drained capers, roughly chopped

2 tablespoons chopped gherkins

2 hard-boiled eggs, finely chopped

1 tablespoon finely chopped anchovies

1 teaspoon kosher salt

1 teaspoon freshly cracked black pepper

2 tablespoons chopped fresh flat-leaf parsley

2 tablespoons thinly sliced fresh chives

Fried Zucchini Flowers

Vegetable oil, for frying

1 cup corn flour

½ cup all-purpose flour

1 teaspoon kosher salt, plus more for seasoning

1½ cups soda water

16 zucchini flowers

1 Make the gribiche sauce: In a large bowl, whisk together the mustard, white balsamic vinegar, olive oil, capers, gherkins, hard-boiled eggs, anchovies, salt, and pepper. Set aside.

2 Deep-fry the zucchini flowers: Line a plate with paper towel. Heat 2 to 3 inches of vegetable oil in a large pot until it reaches 350°F (180°C) on a deep-frying thermometer.

3 Meanwhile, in a medium bowl, combine the corn flour, all-purpose flour, salt, and soda water. Whisk together until it has the consistency of loose pancake batter.

4 Once the oil is hot, begin frying the flowers. Working in batches so you don't crowd the pot, dip the flowers, one at a time, into the batter and let the excess drip back into the bowl. Drop the battered flowers into the hot oil and fry, gently stirring with a slotted spoon so they don't stick together, until lightly golden, about 2 minutes. Transfer the fried flowers to the paper towel to absorb excess oil, then season with salt. Repeat until all the flowers have been deep-fried.

5 Arrange the deep-fried zucchini flowers on a plate. Stir the parsley and chives into the gribiche sauce, then spoon over the flowers. Serve immediately.

Peaches with Blue Cheese and Crispy Prosciutto

Serves 4

Ontario peaches are a classic Québec late-summer staple. I know it sounds weird, but it's true. We look forward to the perfect baskets with little blue cupcake paper to make everything from salads and preserves to pies. Crunchy, creamy, sweet, and salty, this salad has it all.

4 thin slices prosciutto

4 ripe peaches, washed, quartered, and pitted

4 ounces (115 g) crumbly blue cheese

Aged balsamic vinegar, for drizzling

Olive oil, for drizzling

Freshly cracked black pepper

1 Preheat the oven to 375°F (190°C). Line a baking sheet with parchment paper.

2 Lay the prosciutto slices, without overlapping, on the lined baking sheet. Cover with another sheet of parchment paper and place a second baking sheet on top. Bake until the prosciutto has darkened in colour, about 15 minutes. Remove from the oven and lift off the hot baking sheet and the top sheet of parchment paper. Set aside to let the prosciutto cool. After about 7 minutes, the prosciutto will be crispy.

3 Arrange the peaches on a serving plate. Gently crumble or slice the blue cheese and scatter over the peaches. Drizzle with some aged balsamic vinegar and olive oil. Crack some black pepper over top. Gently break up the prosciutto slices and scatter over the top. Serve immediately.

Fried Halloumi and Green Tomatoes with Warm Garlic and Mustard Seed Vinaigrette

Serves 2

Halloumi is a versatile, salty cheese that is very close to a Québec cheese curd. It can be deep-fried, grilled, or roasted, but my favourite way to have it is pan-fried. Frying it slowly creates a crispy caramelized crust and soft, chewy centre. I first made this recipe with unripe tomatoes from my garden, but heirloom green tomatoes or red tomatoes work great.

Warm Garlic and Mustard Seed Vinaigrette

¼ cup olive oil

2 shallots, thinly sliced

4 garlic cloves, smashed and chopped

1 tablespoon yellow mustard seeds

3 tablespoons white balsamic vinegar

Halloumi and Tomatoes

¼ cup vegetable oil

8 ounces (225 g) halloumi cheese, crumbled

3 or 4 ripe green heirloom tomatoes, cut into bite-size wedges

½ teaspoon red chili flakes

¼ cup fresh flat-leaf parsley leaves

1 Make the warm garlic and mustard seed vinaigrette: Heat the olive oil in a small saucepan over medium-low heat. Once the oil is hot, add the shallots and cook for about 2 minutes, stirring a few times, until soft and translucent. Add the garlic and mustard seeds and cook for another minute, stirring often. Add the white balsamic vinegar and bring to a boil. Once it reaches a boil, remove from the heat and set aside.

2 Fry the halloumi and assemble: Line a plate with paper towel. Heat the vegetable oil in a medium nonstick frying pan over medium-high heat. Once the oil is hot, add the halloumi and fry, gently stirring a few times, until golden brown all over, about 2 minutes. Remove the halloumi from the hot oil and transfer it to the paper towel to soak up excess oil.

3 Arrange the tomato wedges on a serving plate. If the vinaigrette has cooled, return it to the heat. Once it is warm, spoon the vinaigrette all over the tomatoes. Scatter over the halloumi, sprinkle with chili flakes, and garnish with the parsley leaves.

Tomato Pie

Serves 4 to 6

This recipe is a family tradition I stole from my mom or maybe my aunt!? Honestly, I'm not sure who anymore, I just know it's delicious and simple, and can be made in under 30 minutes. Using the summer's ripest tomatoes from the garden is best, but any time of the year works, since baking the tomatoes brings out their flavour. This can be served for brunch, dinner, or as a canapé.

1 sheet (8 ounces/225 g) frozen puff pastry, thawed

1½ tablespoons Dijon mustard

½ cup finely grated Grana Padano cheese

2 to 3 large tomatoes, cut into ¼-inch-thick slices

1 tablespoon fresh thyme leaves

Flaky sea salt

Freshly cracked black pepper

Olive oil, for drizzling

1 Preheat the oven to 375°F (190°C). Line a baking sheet with parchment paper.

2 On a lightly floured work surface, use a rolling pin to roll out the pastry just so it's slightly larger than it was, about an inch more on each side. Carefully roll up the pastry over your rolling pin, then unroll it onto the lined baking sheet. Using a paring knife, cut a shallow 1-inch border on all sides, being careful not to cut through the pastry. Prick the pastry all over with a fork, staying within the border.

3 Brush the pastry with the mustard and sprinkle with the cheese, again staying within the border. Lay the slices of tomato evenly over the cheese. Sprinkle evenly with the thyme and season with salt and a few cracks of pepper. Drizzle evenly with olive oil. Bake until the crust is golden brown, 30 to 35 minutes. Let cool on the baking sheet for about 5 minutes, then cut and serve.

Creamed Corn

Creamed corn is a classic that reminds me of my childhood. I was never sure what was in those cans, but I remember it being delicious. This from-scratch version is more work than opening a can, but its creamy, buttery sweetness is a fine reward.

3 tablespoons salted butter

½ cup finely chopped yellow onion

4 garlic cloves, smashed and roughly chopped

8 sweet corn cobs, shucked and kernels removed

1 teaspoon kosher salt

½ teaspoon white pepper

2 cups heavy (35%) cream

¼ teaspoon smoked paprika

Freshly cracked black pepper

1 Melt the butter in a large pot over medium heat. Once the butter begins to foam, add the onion and cook, stirring often, until translucent, 2 to 3 minutes. Add the garlic and cook for another minute. Add the corn, salt, and white pepper and cook for another minute. Pour in the cream and bring to a simmer, then reduce the heat to medium-low and simmer, stirring occasionally, until the mixture is thick and creamy, about 7 minutes.

2 Serve with a sprinkle of paprika and some freshly cracked black pepper.

Brown Butter
Mashed Potatoes

Funny how one ingredient can totally change with just a little heat. It's hard not to put brown butter on and in everything—I dare you! And everyone knows potatoes and butter are a match made in heaven, especially brown butter with crispy little caramelized bits.

3 pounds (1.35 kg) Yukon Gold potatoes, scrubbed

1½ cups whole milk, warmed

4 tablespoons salted butter, at room temperature

2 teaspoons kosher salt

Freshly cracked black pepper

¼ cup warm Brown Butter (page 255)

1 Using a paring knife, make a very shallow cut all the way around each potato. This will make peeling the skins off easier after cooking. Place the potatoes in a large pot, cover them with water, and bring to a boil over high heat. Reduce the heat to medium, tightly cover with a lid, and simmer for about 20 minutes, until the potatoes are soft and cooked through. Drain the potatoes and let sit until cool enough to handle.

2 Peel the potatoes by pulling the skin at both ends. Pass the potatoes through a ricer back into the pot. (If you don't have a ricer, mash the skinned potatoes in the pot.) Pour in the warm milk and add the butter, salt, and pepper to taste. Stir until the milk and butter are absorbed.

3 Drizzle warm brown butter over the mashed potatoes and serve.

French Fries

One of my many guilty pleasures is fries, and real deep-fried french fries are hard to beat. Actually, they *can't* be beat. From fast food to slow food, frozen, fresh, hand-cut or not, they're amazing! I consider these ones perfect—great taste, no frying, and guaranteed to hit the spot.

6 large russet potatoes, scrubbed

5 cups water

2 cups white vinegar

3 tablespoons vegetable oil

Kosher salt

Freshly cracked black pepper

For serving

Garlic Mayonnaise (page 257)

Ketchup (page 260) or store-bought

1 Square off the potatoes by cutting a little slice off each side and a bit off each end. You should have a rounded rectangle. (This stabilizes the potato and makes it easier to cut into fry shapes.) Cut the potatoes lengthwise into ¼-inch-thick sticks. Place the potato sticks in a large bowl and rinse under cold water. Drain the potatoes, then cover them with the water and white vinegar and let them soak (no need to cover) for at least 4 hours on the counter or overnight in the fridge. (Soaking the potatoes with vinegar will give them a nice briny flavour once cooked.)

2 When you are ready to bake the fries, preheat the oven to 425°F (220°C). Line a baking sheet with parchment paper.

3 Drain the potato sticks and pat dry with paper towel. Wipe out the bowl and in it toss the potatoes with the vegetable oil. Evenly spread the potatoes on the lined baking sheet. Season to taste with salt and pepper. Bake for 20 minutes, then turn the fries over and continue to bake until golden and crispy, about another 15 minutes.

4 Serve the french fries with garlic mayo and ketchup for dipping.

Potato Risotto

I'm not one to make grandiose statements, but potatoes are the best food in the world. Okay, maybe second best after eggs. But when life gives you potatoes, the options are limitless. Here's one of them.

This is my ode to the versatility of the potato, one of my favourite foods to eat and cook with. This recipe is a fun twist on risotto, and my kids love to make and eat it. Slowly cook the potatoes until they're fully cooked but still firm with some bite and super creamy like a perfect risotto. Simple and fast, this makes a great last-minute side dish.

4 cups vegetable stock

2 tablespoons olive oil

1 medium yellow onion, diced

3 garlic cloves, smashed and chopped

8 cups diced peeled Yukon Gold potatoes

1½ tablespoons fresh thyme leaves

1 tablespoon kosher salt

1 teaspoon freshly cracked black pepper

5 tablespoons salted butter

1 cup grated Grana Padano cheese, plus more for garnish

1 In a medium saucepan, bring the vegetable stock to a simmer.

2 Heat the olive oil in a medium pot over medium-high heat. Once the oil is hot, add the onions and cook for about a minute, until soft and translucent. Add the garlic and cook for another 30 seconds, stirring constantly. Add the potatoes, thyme, salt, and pepper and stir well to combine. Reduce the heat to medium-low.

3 Add 1 cup of the simmering vegetable stock to the potatoes and simmer gently, stirring, until most of the stock is absorbed, 3 to 4 minutes. Repeat, adding 1 cup of stock at a time and stirring until the potatoes are soft and creamy but not falling apart, 15 to 20 minutes total. You may not need all the stock. Add the butter and cheese and stir until both are fully incorporated. Remove from the heat and adjust the seasoning.

4 Serve the potato risotto with a little more cheese over top.

Pasta and Pizza

Pesto Pappardelle

Serves 4

I used to spend all my days in the kitchen of my restaurant, but now that I have two young boys and an ever-evolving career, I'm not as hands-on at the restaurant anymore. Nowadays, instead of cooking with the team at work, I mostly cook with my kids. This is the first recipe that I made with them from scratch—the pasta and the pesto—and it's become a family classic.

2¼ cups all-purpose flour

3 large eggs

2 tablespoons olive oil

2 tablespoons water

1 teaspoon kosher salt

¼ cup Pesto (page 259)

Freshly grated Grana Padano cheese

Freshly cracked black pepper

1 Make the pasta dough and shape: Measure the flour into a large bowl. Make a well in the centre of the flour. Add the eggs, olive oil, water, and salt to the well and mix together with a fork until a shaggy dough forms.

2 Turn the dough out onto a floured work surface. Using your hands, knead the dough until it is smooth and elastic, about 3 minutes. Wrap the dough in plastic wrap and let it rest in the fridge for at least 30 minutes.

3 Cut the rested dough into 2 equal portions, cover with a damp kitchen towel, and let rest on the counter for 5 minutes. On a floured work surface, working with one piece of dough at a time, use a floured rolling pin to roll out the dough into a rectangle as best you can, until it is 1/12 inch thick. (Alternatively, you can use a pasta machine to roll out the dough to 1/12 inch thick.)

recipe continues

4 With a short side facing you, dust the dough lightly with flour and roll it up into a loose log. Using a sharp knife, cut the log crosswise into 1-inch-wide strips. Unroll the strips and stretch them by pulling each one lightly through your fingers. Sprinkle the pasta strips with flour and form into loose nests on a floured baking sheet. Repeat with the second ball of dough. The nests can be cooked immediately or stored in the fridge in an airtight container for up to 1 day. Alternatively, you can leave the nests on the baking sheet to dry completely, then store them in an airtight container at room temperature for up to 1 week.

5 Cook the pasta and finish: Bring a large pot of salted water to a boil. Add the pasta and cook for 3 to 4 minutes or until al dente. Drain the pasta.

6 Return the cooked pasta to the pot. Add the pesto and mix well until all the pasta is coated. Divide between shallow bowls and top with freshly grated cheese and a few cracks of black pepper.

7

8

9

10

11

12

Mushroom Risotto

Serves 4 to 6

Fancy dinner on a budget! All the ingredients in this recipe are likely already in your pantry, and you probably have an old chunk of cheese in the fridge. Always keep dried mushrooms on hand to make a great broth in a flash, then all you need is some rice and 20 minutes. My kids make this dish from A to Z with almost no help!

Mushroom Stock

½ cup assorted dried wild mushrooms (such as oyster, portobello, and porcini)

1 garlic clove, smashed

2 sprigs fresh thyme

8 cups boiling water

Risotto

3 tablespoons olive oil, divided

1 small yellow onion, diced

2 garlic cloves, grated on a microplane

5 tablespoons salted butter, divided

1½ cups carnaroli rice

½ cup freshly grated Pecorino Romano cheese

Kosher salt

Freshly cracked black pepper

1 Make the mushroom stock: Place the mushrooms, garlic, and thyme in a large bowl. Pour the boiling water over them and let sit for at least 20 minutes to rehydrate the mushrooms. Strain the stock into another bowl and set aside. Discard the garlic and thyme. Roughly chop the mushrooms and set aside.

2 Make the risotto: Heat 1 tablespoon of the olive oil in a large Dutch oven over medium heat. Once the oil is hot, toss in the onions and cook, stirring occasionally, until soft and translucent, about 2 minutes. Make sure the onions do not brown. Add the garlic and cook for another minute.

3 Reduce the heat to medium-low. Add 1 tablespoon of the butter and the rice and cook, stirring constantly, 1 to 2 minutes, until the rice becomes pale and golden. (This will toast the rice and give it a slightly nutty flavour.) Add about ½ cup of the mushroom stock and cook, stirring every minute, until the stock is completely absorbed. Continue adding the mushroom stock, ½ cup at a time, stirring until all the liquid is absorbed before adding more, until the rice is al dente and the risotto is creamy, 18 to 20 minutes total. You may not need all the stock.

4 Remove the pot from the heat and stir in the chopped mushrooms, the remaining 4 tablespoons butter, and the cheese. Season to taste with salt and pepper. To serve, divide among bowls and drizzle with the remaining 2 tablespoons olive oil.

Ricotta Gnocchi with Lemon and Fresh Peas

Serves 4 to 6

My kids don't come to the restaurant so much anymore. School gets in the way of washing dishes! But when they were toddlers, they'd come by during the day to snack on fried shallots, use the spray nozzle in the dish pit, and eat gnocchi. Nowadays we love to make gnocchi at home. Seared to a crisp on the outside and light and fluffy on the inside, and topped with butter, green peas, and lemon zest, it's the perfect balance, rich but light. It's fun to make and even more fun to eat.

1 cup ricotta cheese, drained

2 large eggs, lightly beaten

½ cup grated Parmigiano-Reggiano cheese

1½ teaspoons kosher salt

1 teaspoon freshly cracked black pepper

1¼ cups all-purpose flour

3 tablespoons olive oil, divided

4 tablespoons salted butter

1 cup thinly sliced shallots

2 garlic cloves, smashed and finely chopped

1½ cups shelled fresh peas (about 1½ pounds/675 g unshelled fresh peas)

1 lemon, for zesting

1 tablespoon thinly sliced fresh mint leaves

1 Make the dough: In a large bowl, mix together the ricotta, eggs, cheese, salt, and pepper.

2 Sift in about ¼ cup of the flour and mix until it is absorbed. Add more flour, a little at a time, mixing after each addition, until all the flour has been added. Once a dough forms, remove it from the bowl and place on a lightly floured work surface. Using your hands, gently knead the dough 2 or 3 times, then wrap it in plastic wrap and let it rest in the fridge for 30 minutes.

3 Shape the gnocchi: After 30 minutes, divide the dough into 6 equal portions. Working with one piece of dough at a time, on a floured work surface, use your hands to roll it out into a rope about ½ inch thick. Using a sharp knife, cut the dough crosswise into 1-inch-wide pillows and place them on a floured baking sheet. Repeat with the remaining pieces of dough. Cover with a kitchen towel and place the gnocchi in the fridge until ready to cook.

4 Cook the gnocchi and finish: Preheat the oven to 150°F (65°C) and line a baking sheet with parchment paper. Bring a large pot of salted water to a boil.

recipe continues

5 Drop the gnocchi into the boiling water. Once most of the gnocchi have floated to the top, cook for another 2 minutes. Drain the gnocchi, reserving ¼ cup of the cooking water.

6 Heat 1 tablespoon of the olive oil in a large frying pan over medium-high heat. Working in batches, add some of the gnocchi to the hot oil and sear on one side only for 1 to 2 minutes, until golden brown on the bottom. Transfer the seared gnocchi to the lined baking sheet and keep warm in the oven while you sear the remaining gnocchi, adding more olive oil between batches.

7 To the same pan (no need to wipe it) over medium-high heat, add the butter. Once the butter is melted and foaming, add the shallots and cook, stirring often, until soft, 1 to 2 minutes. Add the garlic and peas and cook for another 30 seconds. Add the reserved cooking water, increase the heat to high, and bring to a boil. Once the cooking water has mostly reduced and the peas are bright green, remove from the heat.

8 Divide the gnocchi between shallow bowls and spoon the sauce over them. Zest the lemon over the gnocchi and sprinkle with the mint.

Lobster Diavolo

This special-occasion recipe is inspired by one at my favourite restaurant in Portland, Maine, called Street and Co. It's the ultimate date-night meal for Sabrina and me. And it's still the one little thing that we haven't shared with the kids yet. I make it occasionally at home because you can't always make a trip to Portland to eat Lobster Diavolo!

    This is a dish for two people that's served in a big bowl piled with lobster, mussels, clams, shrimp, and tomatoey pasta. It's spicy and messy, and you can help yourself directly from the bowl. It's the ultimate first-date dish because if you survive eating this sloppy treat in front of one another without breaking up, it's a good sign that you'll be able to handle the messier moments in the relationship!

1½ tablespoons olive oil

1 medium yellow onion, finely diced

4 garlic cloves, smashed

1 tablespoon drained capers, chopped

3 anchovy fillets, finely chopped

1 can (14 ounces/398 mL) crushed tomatoes

1 cup bomba calabrese or your favourite hot pepper spread

½ cup water

1 (2-pound/900 g) live lobster

½ pound (225 g) fresh pasta clams, rinsed

½ pound (225 g) fresh mussels, scrubbed and beards removed

½ pound (225 g) peeled Nordic shrimp

½ pound (225 g) linguine

1 lemon, for zesting

1 tablespoon chopped fresh flat-leaf parsley

1 Bring a large pot of salted water to a boil.

2 Meanwhile, prepare the sauce. Heat the olive oil in a large braiser over medium-high heat. Once the oil is hot, add the onions and cook, stirring every 30 seconds, until soft and translucent, 2 to 3 minutes. Reduce the heat to medium, toss in the garlic, capers, and anchovies, and cook for another 2 minutes. Add the crushed tomatoes, bomba calabrese, and water and stir. Increase the heat to high and bring to a boil, then reduce the heat to medium-low. Remove the elastic from the claws of the lobster, add the lobster to the sauce, cover with a lid, and cook for another 10 to 15 minutes, until the antennae easily pull off. Remove the lobster and set aside to cool.

3 Increase the heat to medium, drop in the clams, cover with the lid, and cook for 1 minute. Add the mussels and shrimp, cover, and cook for another 3 to 5 minutes, stirring every minute.

4 Once all the clams and mussels are open, turn off the heat. Discard any clams or mussels that did not open.

recipe continues

5 While the shellfish is cooking, cut the lobster in half and remove the digestive tract from the tail. Crack the claws and knuckles and separate them from the body.

6 Once the shellfish are cooked, return the cracked lobster to the tomato sauce. Add the linguine to the boiling water and cook for 1 minute shy of al dente. Drain the pasta, reserving 1 cup of the cooking water. Add the reserved cooking water to the sauce and bring to a simmer. Add the drained pasta and cook it in the sauce until al dente, 1 to 2 minutes. Transfer to a large bowl. Zest the lemon over the dish and sprinkle with the parsley.

Bar Clam Pasta

Serves 2

I've been going to Prince Edward Island every September for many years. I love everything about the region, but my favourite must be bar clams. They're the largest clams found in the northwest Atlantic, and they're usually found on sandy bottoms at low tide. People steam them, chop the meat up, and jar them with the cooking liquid. This liquid is also known as clam liquor and has such a rich concentrated clam flavour. The second I discovered bar clams they became an essential in my pantry. They are large and meaty, which makes them perfect for chowders and pasta, and are usually even better than fresh clams.

Olive oil

½ cup diced shallots

1 garlic clove, smashed and chopped

1 jar (153 g) Atlantic bar clams, drained and finely chopped, juice reserved

8 ounces (225 g) spaghetti

3 tablespoons salted butter

1 tablespoon chopped fresh flat-leaf parsley

Freshly cracked black pepper

1 Bring a large pot of salted water to a boil.

2 Meanwhile, heat a splash of olive oil in a medium frying pan over medium-high heat. Once the oil is hot, toss in the shallots and cook, stirring occasionally, until soft and translucent, 2 to 3 minutes. Add the garlic and cook for another minute. Pour in the reserved clam juice and continue cooking until reduced by half. Remove from the heat.

3 Add the pasta to the boiling water and cook until 1 to 2 minutes shy of al dente. (The pasta will finish cooking in the sauce.) Drain the pasta, reserving ½ cup of the cooking water.

4 Return the drained pasta and the reserved cooking water to the pot. Pour in the shallot and clam juice mixture and bring to a boil to finish cooking the pasta. Once most of the liquid has been absorbed by the pasta, remove from the heat. Add the chopped clams, butter, and parsley and stir to make a smooth and creamy sauce. Divide between shallow bowls and top with a few cracks of black pepper.

Tuna Bolognese

Serves 4 to 6

Everybody has a childhood memory of mom's spaghetti, and every family has its own version. This is our version, and everything is probably in your pantry. It's inexpensive and quick to throw together, and tastes like you've been cooking for hours. My kids like radiatore pasta with this rich, thick sauce, but you can use whatever pasta you have on hand.

1½ tablespoons olive oil

1 medium yellow onion, finely diced

4 garlic cloves, smashed and chopped

2 teaspoons red chili flakes

1 can (28 ounces/796 mL) crushed tomatoes

¼ cup bomba calabrese or your favourite hot pepper spread

2 cans (170 g each) tuna packed in water

3 bay leaves

4 fresh basil leaves, plus more for garnish

Cooked pasta of choice

1 lemon, for zesting

1 Heat the olive oil in a large pot over medium-high heat. Once the oil is hot, add the onions and cook, stirring occasionally, until soft and translucent, 2 to 3 minutes. Add the garlic and chili flakes and cook for another minute, stirring occasionally. Add the tomatoes, bomba calabrese, tuna with its water, bay leaves, and basil. Bring to a boil, then reduce the heat to low, cover with a lid, and simmer for 60 to 90 minutes, until slightly thickened. Discard the bay leaves.

2 Mix a bit of sauce with your cooked pasta, then divide the pasta between shallow bowls. Pour a generous ladle of sauce over top. Garnish with a few basil leaves and finish with a bit of lemon zest.

Lamb Ragu with Conchiglioni

Serves 4

This recipe was a customer favourite at the restaurant during Covid. Having to reinvent the way we did business and focusing on takeout, delivery, and changing our menu was a challenge, but we made it through. People wanted comforting food that wasn't going to break the bank, and when we put this ragu on the menu, customers really went for it. I brought this pasta home a lot, it was that good—rich, with a hint of that distinct lamb but not too overpowering. Now, it's part of a cast of revolving dishes.

1½ tablespoons olive oil

1 pound (450 g) ground lamb

1 medium yellow onion, finely diced

2 ounces (55 g) pancetta, thinly sliced

4 garlic cloves, smashed and roughly chopped

1 sprig fresh rosemary

3 bay leaves

3 cans (5.5 ounces/156 mL each) tomato paste

6 cups water

1 tablespoon kosher salt

½ teaspoon freshly cracked black pepper

18 ounces (500 g) conchiglioni (large pasta shells)

Grated Grana Padano cheese, for serving

1 Heat the olive oil in a large Dutch oven over medium-high heat. Once the oil is hot, add the lamb, break it apart with a wooden spoon, and cook, stirring often, until browned. Using a slotted spoon, remove the lamb from the pot and transfer to a plate, leaving the fat in the pot. Reduce the heat to medium-low, toss in the onions and pancetta, and cook, stirring occasionally, until the onions start to brown, about 5 minutes. Add the garlic, rosemary, and bay leaves and cook, stirring occasionally, for another 2 minutes.

2 Return the browned lamb and any juices to the pot. Add the tomato paste and cook, stirring constantly, for 2 minutes. Add the water, salt, and pepper and stir well to combine everything. Increase the heat to high and bring the sauce to a boil, then reduce the heat to low, cover with the lid slightly ajar, and simmer, stirring occasionally, for 3 to 4 hours, until the sauce has thickened. Discard the rosemary sprig and bay leaves. (The sauce is even better the next day. You can completely cool the sauce and store in an airtight container in the fridge for up to 1 week.)

3 When the sauce is done, bring a large pot of salted water to a boil. Once the water is boiling, add the pasta and cook until al dente. Drain the pasta, transfer to a large bowl, and mix with a ladleful of the sauce so it doesn't stick together. Divide the pasta between bowls. Top with more sauce and the grated cheese.

Sausage and Pepperoni Lasagna

Serves 8 to 10

Every time I make this lasagna, my biggest challenge is to not eat all the sauce! But I need to come clean: I had never made a lasagna in my life before having kids. I used to cook so much at the restaurant that I rarely cooked at home. My boys forced me to become a home cook, and now it's part of my everyday life. The kids were always having lasagna elsewhere and they begged me to do one at home. So I caved, and I haven't looked back. This is a simple recipe, and the key is in the sauce. The sausage and peperoni in the sauce add a lot of texture, spice, and amazing flavour.

Tomato Sauce

6 Italian sausages (about 1½ pounds/675 g total)

2 tablespoons olive oil

14 ounces (400 g) ½-inch-thick sliced pepperoni

1 medium yellow onion, finely diced

6 garlic cloves, smashed and chopped

2 cans (13 ounces/369 mL each) tomato paste

8 cups water

1½ tablespoons kosher salt

1 teaspoon freshly cracked black pepper

6 large fresh basil leaves

For assembly

1 package (13.25 ounces/375 g) oven-ready lasagna noodles

2 batches Béchamel Sauce (page 256), warmed

½ pound (225 g) fresh baby spinach

2½ pounds (1.125 kg) mozzarella cheese, grated (9 cups)

1 Make the tomato sauce: Remove the sausage from the casing. Pinch the sausages into chunks as if you were making small meatballs.

2 Heat the olive oil in a large pot over medium-high heat. Once the oil is hot, working in batches so you do not crowd the pot, add the sausage and pepperoni and sear, stirring often, for 2 to 3 minutes, until lightly browned all over. Transfer the cooked sausage and pepperoni to a plate. Cook the remaining sausage and pepperoni.

3 To the same pot (no need to wipe it), add the onions and cook, stirring occasionally, until soft and translucent, 3 to 5 minutes. Toss in the garlic and cook for another minute, stirring constantly.

4 Add the tomato paste and cook, stirring constantly, for 2 minutes. Increase the heat to high. Add the water, salt, pepper, and basil and bring to a boil, stirring occasionally. Once the sauce is boiling, add the seared sausage and pepperoni, then reduce the heat to low, cover with a lid, and simmer for 2½ hours, stirring occasionally. The sauce can be made ahead of time. Let cool, then store in an airtight container in the fridge for up to 5 days.

recipe continues

5 Assemble and bake the lasagna: Fifteen minutes before the sauce is done, preheat the oven to 350°F (180°C).

6 Using a slotted spoon, remove the sausage and pepperoni from the tomato sauce and set aside.

7 Ladle a little more than a cup of the tomato sauce into a 13 × 9-inch baking dish and spread it out to completely cover the bottom. Top with a layer of lasagna sheets. Evenly top the lasagna sheets with a third of the béchamel sauce, then a third of the spinach, and then a quarter of the cheese. Arrange a third of the sausage and pepperoni mixture over the cheese and top with about a quarter of the remaining tomato sauce. Repeat this process two more times. Finally, top with another layer of lasagna sheets, the remaining tomato sauce, then the remaining cheese.

8 Bake the lasagna for 40 minutes. Increase the oven temperature to 450°F (230°C) and bake for another 10 to 15 minutes, until the top is golden brown. Let cool for at least 20 minutes before serving. Leftover lasagna can be stored, covered, in the fridge for up to 5 days. Reheat in a 350°F (180°C) oven for 15 to 20 minutes, until crispy on top.

Pizza Dough

Pizza is the ultimate food. It's simple, it usually has all food groups, and it can be topped with almost anything. Even if it's not great, it's still pretty good! And what's more, anybody can make it at home. This is my no-fail recipe for the pizzaiolo in all of us. In a wood-burning, gas-burning, or traditional oven, it's just about having fun perfecting the art of zaa. And remember, *piano piano* ("take it easy") on the toppings—less is more!

1½ cups warm water

3 teaspoons granulated sugar

2 teaspoons active dry yeast

3½ cups all-purpose flour

2 teaspoons kosher salt

2 tablespoons olive oil

1 In a medium bowl, whisk together the water, sugar, and yeast. Let sit until the yeast begins to foam, 5 to 7 minutes.

2 In a separate medium bowl, stir together the flour and salt.

3 When the yeast is active, stir the olive oil into the yeast mixture. Add the yeast mixture to the flour mixture and mix with a wooden spoon until a sticky dough forms.

4 Turn the dough out onto a lightly floured work surface. Using your hands, knead for about 5 minutes, until smooth and spongy. Place the dough in an oiled large bowl, cover the bowl with a damp kitchen towel, and let the dough rest on the counter until doubled in size, about 45 minutes.

5 Turn the dough out onto an unfloured work surface. Using a dough scraper or sharp knife, cut the dough into 3 equal pieces. Using your hands, shape each piece into a ball. Place the dough balls in a baking dish large enough to fit them, cover with a kitchen towel, then transfer to the fridge and let the dough rest for 25 minutes before rolling out. (The dough can be stored, wrapped in plastic wrap, in the fridge for up to 3 days or in a resealable plastic bag in the freezer for up to 2 months.)

For toppings and baking instructions, see the pizza variation recipes on pages 136 to 138.

Pizza Variations

Pepperoni Pizza

1 ball of Pizza Dough (page 135)

½ cup pizza sauce

¾ cup grated mozzarella cheese

10 to 12 slices pepperoni

1 Preheat the oven to 450°F (230°C). (If using a pizza oven, preheat to 600°F/315°C.)

2 Lightly flour your work surface. Dust the dough ball with flour, then use a rolling pin to roll out the dough into a 9-inch circle (it doesn't have to be perfect).

3 If using an electric or gas oven: Place the dough on a 10-inch perforated pizza pan. Spread the pizza sauce evenly over the dough, leaving a ½-inch border. Sprinkle the cheese evenly over the sauce. Scatter the pepperoni over top. Bake for 10 to 12 minutes, until the crust has puffed and is golden brown.

OR

4 If using a pizza oven: Place the dough on a very lightly floured pizza peel. Spread the pizza sauce evenly over the dough, leaving a ½-inch border. Sprinkle the cheese evenly over the sauce. Scatter the pepperoni over top. Carefully slide the peel into the pizza oven, tilt the tip of the peel towards the bottom of the oven, and quickly pull back on the peel, allowing the pizza to slide onto the hot deck. Bake for 2 to 3 minutes, turning the pizza halfway through using a metal pizza peel, until the crust has puffed and has charred spots. Carefully remove the pizza from the oven using a metal pizza peel. Let cool for 2 minutes before cutting.

Mushroom Pizza

1 ball of Pizza Dough (page 135)

1 batch Mornay Sauce (page 255)

½ cup sliced cremini mushrooms

½ cup grated Grana Padano cheese

1 teaspoon fresh thyme leaves

1 Preheat the oven to 450°F (230°C). (If using a pizza oven, preheat to 600°F/315°C.)

2 Lightly flour your work surface. Dust the dough ball with flour, then use a rolling pin to roll out the dough into a 9-inch circle (it doesn't have to be perfect).

3 If using an electric or gas oven: Place the dough on a 10-inch perforated pizza pan. Spread the mornay sauce evenly over the dough, leaving a ½-inch border. Scatter the mushrooms evenly over the sauce. Sprinkle with the cheese and thyme. Bake for 10 to 12 minutes, until the crust has puffed and is golden brown.

OR

4 If using a pizza oven: Place the dough on a very lightly floured pizza peel. Spread the mornay sauce evenly over the dough, leaving a ½-inch border. Scatter the mushrooms evenly over the sauce. Sprinkle with the cheese and thyme. Carefully slide the peel into the pizza oven, tilt the tip of the peel towards the bottom of the oven, and quickly pull back on the peel, allowing the pizza to slide onto the hot deck. Bake for 2 to 3 minutes, turning the pizza halfway through using a metal pizza peel, until the crust has puffed and has charred spots. Carefully remove the pizza from the oven using a metal pizza peel. Let cool for 2 minutes before cutting.

Pesto and Fresh Mozzarella Pizza

1 ball of Pizza Dough (page 135)

3 tablespoons Pesto (page 259)

1 ball fresh buffalo mozzarella

Freshly cracked black pepper

Olive oil, for drizzling

1 Preheat the oven to 450°F (230°C). (If using a pizza oven, preheat to 600°F/315°C.)

2 Lightly flour your work surface. Dust the dough ball with flour, then use a rolling pin to roll out the dough into a 9-inch circle (it doesn't have to be perfect).

3 **If using an electric or gas oven:** Place the dough on a 10-inch perforated pizza pan. Spread the pesto evenly over the dough, leaving a ½-inch border. Tear the mozzarella and scatter it over the pesto. Crack some black pepper all over and drizzle with some olive oil. Bake for 10 to 12 minutes, until the crust has puffed and is golden brown.

OR

4 **If using a pizza oven:** Place the dough on a very lightly floured pizza peel. Spread the pesto evenly over the dough, leaving a ½-inch border. Tear the mozzarella and scatter it over the pesto. Crack some black pepper all over and drizzle with some olive oil. Carefully slide the peel into the pizza oven, tilt the tip of the peel towards the bottom of the oven, and quickly pull back on the peel, allowing the pizza to slide onto the hot deck. Bake for 2 to 3 minutes, turning the pizza halfway through using a metal pizza peel, until the crust has puffed and has charred spots. Carefully remove the pizza from the oven using a metal pizza peel. Let cool for 2 minutes before cutting.

Fish and Seafood

Shucking Oysters

So you've got your perfect fresh oysters and you've gathered a crowd. Now let's get shucking! Take your time, enjoy the moment, and try to present the best-looking oyster possible. That means trying as much as possible to not break the flesh. A broken oyster has no effect on flavour, it just doesn't look quite as appealing.

You'll need crushed ice for serving, a clean, well-organized work surface, a stable cutting board, clean kitchen towels, and a sharp oyster knife that's comfortable and easy to handle. You can easily find an oyster knife at a fishmonger or in the fish section of a grocery store.

Oysters are shaped like teardrops. The hinge is at the top of the narrow part and that is where the oyster knife goes in to pop the shell open. Here are some basic steps to shuck your own oysters:

1. Spread ice on a serving platter to hold the oysters in place.

2. Put a folded kitchen towel on your work surface. Place an oyster, flat side up, in the centre of the towel, then fold the towel over the wide part of the oyster to shield your fingers in case the knife slips.

3. Holding the oyster steady with the towel, work the oyster knife into the hinge without forcing it. Once you secure the knife in the hinge, twist it up and down to pop the top shell up. Using your fingertip, hold open the oyster where you popped it open. Remove your knife and clean off any mud or pieces of shell.

4. Keeping the oyster level so you don't lose that delicious liquor, slide the knife back in, keeping it flat against the top shell, and scrape underneath the shell to release the small muscle that holds the shell in place. Discard the top shell. Next, slide the knife under the oyster and scrape the bottom shell to release the muscle on the bottom that holds the oyster in place.

5. Use the oyster knife to remove any pieces of shell that are visible, and nestle the oyster in its half shell on ice. Repeat with the remaining oysters. Serve with lemon wedges, hot sauce, cocktail sauce, grated fresh horseradish, and my three mignonettes (pages 147 to 148). The acidity and textures of the mignonettes compliment briny oysters perfectly.

Oysters with Mignonettes

I love the sense of mystery about oysters, the briny seawater flavour, and the fact that every oyster is unique. But there's no way around it—you have to pry the meat out one oyster at a time!

Shucking oysters is actually simple and can be mastered by anyone who wants to learn (see Shucking Oysters, page 145). Some people just like to eat them, and that's okay too! I suggest you buy a case of oysters with some friends or family and make it an event. There's always someone who has never had one or has never shucked one, so not only are they delicious, but it's a great way to have a party!

It's crucial to find the freshest and best quality oysters. So how do you know if your oysters are fresh? First, make sure to visit a reputable fishmonger to steer you in the right direction. Second, the case should have a harvesting date on it. Third, sniff it! Usually there's no in-between when an oyster is bad—you'll smell it right away. A fresh oyster smells briny like the ocean. Fourth, a fresh oyster should always be fully closed. Fifth, if you tap on it with another oyster, it should sound full. If it sounds hollow, like there's no meat in it, that's a red flag, so get rid of it. Finally, good oysters are never dried out. They're plump, firm, and juicy. When in doubt just throw out! If you are not immediately shucking your oysters, store them in the fridge with a damp kitchen towel over them (not in an airtight container as they need to breathe). Before shucking, give the oysters a quick rinse under cold water.

Always serve oysters on crushed ice—it keeps them cool and holds them in place. Some people use coarse salt, but I find it tends to stick to the shell, so when you slurp the oyster back, you catch some unnecessary salt along with it. You can't go wrong with crushed ice.

Classic Mignonette

⅔ cup red wine vinegar

2 tablespoons finely chopped shallot

1 teaspoon coarsely cracked black pepper

1 In a small bowl, stir together the red wine vinegar, shallots, and pepper and let sit for at least 1 hour before using.

recipe continues

Cucumber Ginger Mignonette

⅔ cup white balsamic vinegar

2 tablespoons finely chopped cucumber

2 tablespoons freshly squeezed lemon juice

½ teaspoon minced peeled fresh ginger

½ teaspoon coarsely cracked black pepper

1 In a small bowl, stir together the white balsamic vinegar, cucumber, lemon juice, ginger, and pepper and let sit for at least 1 hour before using.

Apple Cider Mignonette

⅔ cup apple cider vinegar

1 tablespoon finely chopped apple (I like tart Granny Smith, but any variety is fine)

1 tablespoon finely chopped shallots

¼ teaspoon coarsely cracked black pepper

1 In a small bowl, stir together the apple cider vinegar, apple, shallots, and pepper and let sit for at least 1 hour before using.

Lobster Salad

Serves 4

Welcome to the lighter side of lobster. I have a favourite lobster salad, at Ken's Place near Pine Point Beach in Scarborough, Maine: lobster meat, potato salad, cheese, pickles, green pepper rings—a masterpiece, but it's quite heavy. This is not that, but maybe better with large chunks of perfectly cooked lobster and warm buttered croutons and drizzled with tangy creamy lemon dill dressing! Make sure to freeze the lobster shells to make stock another time.

Lobster Salad

2 (1½ to 2 pounds/675 to 900 g each) live lobsters

1 head romaine lettuce

½ cup thinly sliced red onion

1 cup halved cherry tomatoes

1 cup sliced cucumber

Croutons (recipe below)

¼ cup lemon dill dressing (recipe below)

Croutons

3 tablespoons salted butter

2 tablespoons olive oil

4 cups torn bread

1 tablespoon Old Bay seasoning

Kosher salt

Freshly cracked black pepper

Lemon Dill Dressing

1 cup plain full-fat Greek yogurt

Zest and juice of 1 lemon

2 tablespoons chopped fresh dill

1 garlic clove, minced

1 Prepare the lobster: Fill a large bowl or clean kitchen sink with ice water. (The bowl should be big enough to fit both lobsters.)

2 Fill a large pot with water, season generously with salt, and bring to a boil. Once the water is boiling, remove the elastic from the claws of the lobsters and drop them into the pot. Cover with a lid so the water boils again as quickly as possible. Once the water has returned to a boil, remove the lid and cook the lobsters for 10 to 12 minutes, until the antennae easily pull off. Drop the lobsters into the ice water as soon as they are cooked. Let chill for 5 minutes, then remove them from the water.

4 Cover a cutting board with a kitchen towel, as the lobsters will release liquid when you crack them. Using a pair of kitchen shears, begin cracking the lobster. Remove the meat from the claws, knuckles, and tail. If you want to be meticulous, use a rolling pin to roll out the meat from the little legs: Remove the legs from the body and cut the small claws off. Starting where the leg meets the body, press down and roll over the leg with the rolling pin. A small tube of lobster meat will come out. Put all the meat in a bowl and set aside. (The shells can be used to make lobster stock immediately or frozen for later use.)

recipe continues

5 Make the croutons: Melt the butter in a large frying pan over medium-low heat. Once the butter begins to foam, add the olive oil and the bread. Sprinkle with the Old Bay seasoning, a bit of salt, and a few cracks of pepper and toss everything together to coat the bread. Reduce the heat to low and toast the bread, stirring often, until it is golden brown and crunchy all over but still slightly soft in the middle, 10 to 12 minutes. Transfer the croutons to a plate lined with paper towel and set aside.

6 Make the lemon dill dressing: In a medium bowl, stir together the yogurt, lemon zest and juice, dill, and garlic. Leftover dressing can be stored in an airtight container in the fridge for up to 1 week.

7 Assemble the salad: In a large bowl, toss together the lettuce, red onions, tomatoes, cucumbers, and croutons. Arrange the lobster meat over the salad and drizzle with lemon dill dressing.

Mexican Shrimp Cocktail

Serves 6 to 8

I love Mexico. The people, the surfing, and the food, but mostly the regionality and variety of food in every state. One of my favourite places to eat is in Bucerías, a small town in Nayarit close to Puerto Vallarta. Try Mariscos Villarreal or Mariscos El Toto, run by brothers and across the street from each other. When one is closed the other is open, so go anytime. Their seafood cocktail is made with the freshest seafood, lots of avocado, lime, and cucumber, and served with tostadas, crackers, and tortillas. In my version I like to add cocktail sauce to thicken it up and give it a little extra sweetness and heat from the horseradish.

1 cup diced cucumber

1 cup diced red onion

1 cup diced seeded jalapeño pepper

1 cup diced celery

2 avocados, pitted, peeled, and diced

4 cups peeled Nordic shrimp

Zest and juice of 3 limes

¾ cup chopped cilantro leaves

1 cup cocktail sauce

1 cup tomato juice

For serving

Saltine crackers

Tortilla chips

1 In a large bowl, combine the cucumber, red onions, jalapeños, celery, avocados, shrimp, lime zest and juice, cilantro, cocktail sauce, and tomato juice. Gently mix together.

2 Spoon into cocktail glasses and serve with crackers and tortilla chips.

Shrimp Aspic

This is the most famous and cherished recipe in my family. My grandmother made this for every special occasion and family gathering. The only thing is, it's not an aspic and there is more salmon than shrimp, so "shrimp aspic" may not be the most accurate name, but that's what she called it! My grandma passed away at one hundred years of age and I got the recipe from my uncle. This is my version. Serve it with crackers, crudités, and olives.

2 cans (213 g each) sockeye salmon, drained and juice reserved

8 ounces (225 g) peeled Nordic shrimp

1 cup grated cucumber with its juices

½ cup diced celery

¼ cup finely chopped sweet red pepper

¼ cup finely chopped green onion

½ cup mayonnaise

½ cup sour cream

1 teaspoon bomba calabrese or your favourite hot pepper spread

1 teaspoon dried dill

1 teaspoon kosher salt

Zest and juice of 1 lemon

2 packets (1 tablespoon each) unflavoured powdered gelatin

1 cup boiling water

For serving

Vegetables (such as carrot, celery, and cucumber sticks and halved radishes)

Olives

Saltine crackers

1 Lightly oil the bottom and sides of a 9 × 5-inch loaf pan or similar size mould.

2 In a large bowl, combine the salmon, shrimp, cucumber and its juices, celery, sweet pepper, green onion, mayonnaise, sour cream, bomba calabrese, dill, salt, and lemon zest and juice. Mix well.

3 In a small bowl, combine the gelatin and the reserved salmon juice. Pour in the boiling water and stir until the gelatin is fully dissolved. Add the gelatin mixture to the seafood mixture and mix well.

4 Spoon the mixture into the prepared pan. Cover with plastic wrap and gently press down so the plastic is touching the mixture. Place in the fridge for at least 12 hours or overnight to set.

5 Once the aspic is set, remove the plastic wrap. Run a knife around the edge of the aspic, then place a serving plate upside down over the mould. Hold the mould and the plate together and invert. Gently knock it on the counter to release the aspic from the mould. Serve with veggies, olives, and crackers.

Shrimp Rolls

Makes 6 shrimp rolls

Arctic, or Nordic, shrimp is in season in Québec for only a few weeks in the spring and early summer, but you can find them shelled and frozen all year round. The best way to eat fresh ones is to suck out the eggs, pinch off the head, then peel the shell off the tail. They're delicious but a bit of work. These rolls are a switch-up on a classic lobster roll showcasing one of Gaspésie's finest exports.

1½ pounds (675 g) peeled Nordic shrimp

¼ cup mayonnaise

1 teaspoon flaky sea salt

1 teaspoon freshly cracked black pepper

6 brioche hot dog buns

4 tablespoons salted butter, melted until lightly browned

2 tablespoons thinly sliced fresh chives

1 In a large bowl, gently toss together the shrimp, mayonnaise, salt, and pepper until combined.

2 Slice open the buns. Arrange the buns on a platter and stuff each one with a generous portion of the shrimp mix. Drizzle the melted butter over the shrimp and top with the chives.

Fish Burgers

Makes 4 burgers

Fish burgers are a summer classic at our family cottage. We make our burgers with bass or perch that we catch right off my mom's dock in the Eastern Townships. This is a simple burger, with lettuce and tomato from our garden, tartar sauce, and a touch of dill in the crunchy pickle. Nothing tastes better than catching your dinner!

2 skinless fillets fresh bass, pickerel, or perch (or whatever you catch!), (about 1½ pounds/ 675 g total)

Kosher salt

Freshly cracked black pepper

¼ cup all-purpose flour, for dredging

¼ cup vegetable oil, for frying

4 brioche hamburger buns, split and toasted

¼ cup Tartar Sauce (page 258)

1 cup shredded iceberg lettuce

4 slices Jarlsberg cheese

4 slices tomato

4 slices garlic dill pickles

½ red onion, thinly sliced

1 Prepare and fry the fish burgers: Cut the fillets in half crosswise so each piece fits on a burger bun. Season the fish with salt and pepper. Place the flour on a large plate. Dredge the fish in the flour, just enough to coat. Shake off any excess flour.

2 Line a plate with paper towel. Heat the vegetable oil in a large frying pan over medium-high heat. Working in batches, carefully place the floured fish in the hot oil and fry, turning once, until a golden crust forms, 2 to 3 minutes per side. Once the fish is cooked, remove from the hot oil with a fish spatula and place on the paper towel to absorb excess oil.

3 Assemble the burgers: Spread 1 tablespoon of the tartar sauce on each of the bottom halves of the buns. Layer the shredded iceberg lettuce on top. Place the fish on top of the lettuce, then a slice of cheese. Top with the tomato, pickle, and some red onion. Finish the burgers with the tops and serve.

Salmon Boulettes

Serves 4 to 6

This is my girlfriend Sabrina's recipe, and it can be a lifesaver when you barely have anything left in the fridge. All you need is a can of wild salmon, a sweet potato, and leftover rice. The sweet potato is key: it keeps the fish cakes moist and it gives them a nice colour. These salmon boulettes are a family favourite, and we always serve them with yellow mustard for dipping.

2 small sweet potatoes

1 cup cooked rice

2 cans (213 g each) wild salmon, drained

2 large eggs

2 tablespoons chopped fresh flat-leaf parsley

1 tablespoon kosher salt

1 teaspoon freshly cracked black pepper

2 tablespoons olive oil, for drizzling

Yellow mustard, for dipping

1 Preheat the oven to 375°F (190°C).

2 Prick the sweet potatoes all over with a fork and place them on a baking sheet lined with parchment paper. Bake for 60 to 90 minutes, or until the flesh is soft. Remove from the oven and let sit until cool enough to handle.

3 In a medium bowl, combine the rice, salmon, eggs, parsley, salt, and pepper.

4 Once the sweet potatoes are cool, cut them in half, scoop out the flesh, and add it to the salmon mixture. Mix well. Reserve the baking sheet with a fresh sheet of parchment.

5 Using 2 large spoons, form the batter into quenelles by scooping up about 2 tablespoons of batter and using the other spoon to press it into itself. Transfer the mixture between the 2 spoons a few times to get a nice football shape. It should have three slightly curving sides. Place the quenelles on the lined baking sheet, evenly spaced. Drizzle them with olive oil. Bake for 12 minutes per side, until crispy and golden brown.

6 Serve with mustard on the side for dipping.

Cod Fritters

Makes about 24 fritters

This take on salt cod fritters came about one day when I felt like treating myself but was too lazy to leave the house. It is quick and easy and can be made from standard pantry items. Served with a squeeze of fresh lemon, it always hits the spot when you need a little fried comfort food or a fast canapé for last-minute guests.

1 can (14 ounces/398 mL) chickpeas, rinsed and drained

2 cans (120 g each) cod fillets packed in oil, drained

1 garlic clove, minced

Zest and juice of 1 lemon

1 large egg

2 tablespoons all-purpose flour

1 teaspoon baking powder

1 teaspoon kosher salt

2 cups vegetable oil, for frying

Garlic Mayonnaise (page 257), for serving

1 In a large bowl, combine the chickpeas, cod, garlic, lemon zest and juice, egg, flour, baking powder, and salt. Mash together to form a chunky dough-like mixture.

2 Using 2 large spoons, form the batter into quenelles by scooping up about 2 tablespoons of batter and using the other spoon to press it into itself. Transfer the mixture between the 2 spoons a few times to get a nice football shape. It should have three slightly curving sides. Place the quenelles on a plate.

3 Once all the fritters are formed, line a plate with paper towel. Heat the vegetable oil in a large frying pan over medium-high heat. Test the oil by dropping a bit of batter into the oil. If the batter bubbles up right away, the oil is ready for frying. Working in batches so you don't crowd the pan, carefully lower the fritters into the hot oil and fry until they are golden brown all over, 4 to 5 minutes. Remove the fritters from the hot oil and place them on the paper towel to absorb excess oil. Season with salt. Serve immediately with garlic mayo.

Brown Butter Scallops

Serves 2

To this day, cooking scallops is probably my fondest memory of cooking on the line. There is a satisfaction when the scallops peel off the pan and are perfectly golden brown. Instant reward! With its garlicky caper sweet brown butter, this dish is simple and a great last-minute option, and looks and tastes elegant. No one needs to know it was that easy!

8 sea scallops (U10 size)

Kosher salt

Freshly cracked black pepper

1½ tablespoons vegetable oil

3 tablespoons Brown Butter (page 255)

1 tablespoon drained capers

1 teaspoon finely chopped anchovies

2 garlic cloves, smashed and finely chopped

1 tablespoon chopped flat-leaf parsley

1 Place the scallops on a kitchen towel and pat dry. Season all over with salt and pepper. (When cooking at home, I don't remove the muscle off the side of the scallop. They're a bit chewy, but scallops are expensive so I don't like to waste any.)

2 Heat the vegetable oil in a large heavy frying pan over high heat. Once the oil is very hot, gently place the scallops, bigger side down, in the pan, slightly reduce the heat to medium-high, and sear the scallops on one side for 1 to 2 minutes, until a golden-brown crust has formed. Remove the scallops from the pan and transfer to a plate. Discard the oil (no need to wipe the pan).

3 Return the pan to medium-low heat. Add the brown butter, capers, anchovies, and garlic and cook for about 30 seconds, stirring constantly. Return the scallops, seared side up, to the pan and cook them about another minute, until soft but slightly firm. Remove from the heat.

4 Divide the scallops between plates, spoon the brown butter sauce over them, and serve.

Haddock with Tomatoes

Serves 2

This fresh and light summer dish can be made with any white fish. It's all done in one pan for maximum flavour and easy cleanup. The tomatoes, onions, and butter come together to create an amazing sauce. I like to serve it with warm crusty bread to soak up all the juices.

2 skinless wild Canadian haddock or other white fish fillets

Kosher salt

Freshly cracked black pepper

1 tablespoon olive oil

1 tablespoon salted butter

1 small yellow onion, thinly sliced

1 garlic clove, smashed and finely chopped

1 cup halved cherry tomatoes

1 teaspoon chopped fresh flat-leaf parsley

1 teaspoon chopped fresh rosemary

Juice of ½ lemon

1 Season the haddock with salt and pepper.

2 Heat the olive oil in a large nonstick frying pan over medium-high heat. Once the oil is hot, sear the fish until golden brown on the bottom, 2 to 3 minutes. Gently turn the fillets, add the butter to the pan, and cook for another 3 to 4 minutes, until cooked through. Carefully remove the fish from the pan and place it on a serving platter, reserving the butter and oil in the pan.

3 Add the onions and garlic to the pan and cook, stirring, until the onions are translucent, about 1 minute. Add the tomatoes and cook for another 30 seconds. Remove the pan from the heat and toss in the parsley, rosemary, and lemon juice. Season to taste with salt and pepper. Pour the pan sauce over the fish and serve.

Swordfish Kebobs

Serves 4

My kids love fish and seafood, and this recipe is one of their favourites—and it's always a hit with the adults too. When the kids were younger and developing their palates, it was sometimes a struggle to get them to try new things. Apparently, you can't just eat pasta with ketchup! But that wasn't the case with this recipe. Mild white fish that can be perfectly cut into cubes for the kebobs, a marinade that adds a smoky flavour, and a hint of lemon make this dish irresistible. We love to eat this souvlaki-style, in pitas with tzatziki. (You'll need 8 bamboo sticks; soak while you marinate the fish.)

14 ounces (400 g) swordfish steaks (at least 1½ inches thick), skinned and cut into 1-inch cubes

2 tablespoons olive oil

1 garlic clove, minced

1 teaspoon fresh thyme leaves

1 tablespoon dried dill

1 tablespoon smoked paprika

Pinch of red chili flakes

Zest of 1 lemon

1 teaspoon kosher salt

½ teaspoon freshly cracked black pepper

1 yellow onion, quartered lengthwise and separated into layers

1 pint (2 cups) cherry tomatoes (about 16 tomatoes)

For serving

Tzatziki

Pita Bread (page 43) or store-bought, warmed

1 Place the cubed swordfish in a medium bowl. Add the olive oil, garlic, thyme, dill, paprika, chili flakes, lemon zest, salt, and pepper. Mix well. Cover the bowl tightly with plastic wrap and marinate the fish in the fridge for 1 hour.

2 Meanwhile, soak 8 bamboo skewers in water for at least 1 hour.

3 Prepare the grill for direct cooking over high heat.

4 To assemble the kebobs, alternately thread the marinated swordfish, onion, and tomatoes onto the soaked skewers. Discard the marinade.

5 Grill the kebobs over direct heat until the swordfish is lightly charred and fully cooked, about 3 minutes per side. Serve with tzatziki and warmed pita bread.

Mussel Pot Pie

Serves 4 to 6

Mussels are fun to cook with—fairly inexpensive, available year-round, and delicious!
You get not only great-tasting morsels from Canada's oceans but the most delicate broth.
Topped with flaky, buttery puff pastry it is possibly the best weeknight comfort meal.

Mussels

1 tablespoon olive oil

1 medium yellow onion, finely diced

2 garlic cloves, smashed and chopped

1 teaspoon kosher salt

½ teaspoon freshly cracked black pepper

½ teaspoon red chili flakes

½ teaspoon coarsely ground fennel seeds

4 pounds (1.8 kg) fresh mussels, scrubbed and beards removed

2 cups water

Pot Pie

½ cup salted butter

½ cup all-purpose flour

2½ cups reserved broth from mussels (from above)

½ cup heavy (35%) cream

3 cups frozen mixed vegetables

1 teaspoon kosher salt

Picked mussels (from above)

1 sheet (8 ounces/225 g) frozen puff pastry, thawed

1 large egg, lightly beaten

1 tablespoon flaky sea salt

1 Prepare the mussels: Heat the olive oil in a large pot over high heat. Once the oil is hot, add the onions and cook for 30 seconds, stirring constantly. Add the garlic, kosher salt, pepper, chili flakes, and fennel seeds and cook, stirring, for another 30 seconds. Add the mussels and water, cover with a lid, and steam the mussels until they open, about 2 minutes. Remove the pot from the heat. Using a slotted spoon or spider strainer, carefully remove the mussels, place them in a large bowl, and let sit until cool enough to handle. Reserve the broth. Discard any mussels that did not open.

2 Once the mussels have cooled, pick them from their shells and set aside. Discard the shells.

3 Assemble and bake the pot pie: Preheat the oven to 400°F (200°C).

4 Melt the butter in a large pot over medium heat. Once the butter is melted, reduce the heat to medium-low, add the flour, and cook for 5 minutes, stirring constantly. Pour in the reserved mussel broth and the cream, increase the heat to medium, and continue to stir until thickened and simmering, 10 to 15 minutes Remove the pot from the heat and stir in the reserved mussels, the mixed vegetables, and kosher salt.

5 Pour the mixture into an 8-inch square casserole dish or similar size dish. Unroll the puff pastry and place it over the filling. Gently fold the excess dough over the sides of the casserole dish. Pierce a few holes in the top to allow the steam to escape.

6 Brush the top of the puff pastry with the egg, then sprinkle with the flaky sea salt. Bake until the pastry is puffed and golden brown, 30 to 40 minutes. Let cool for at least 10 minutes before serving.

Seafood Chili

Serves 6 to 8

I could eat shellfish every day! It's my favourite food to eat and my favourite ingredient to cook with. This recipe combines comfort and fresh seafood for a one-bowl meal. I'm not a boat captain, fisherman, or a harvester, but I think that after a long day on the water, this would be the perfect dish to warm up to.

1½ cups dried navy beans

1 tablespoon olive oil

2 medium yellow onions, roughly chopped

4 garlic cloves, smashed and chopped

½ leek (white and light green parts only), thinly sliced

¾ cup chopped celery hearts

2 tablespoons kosher salt

1 teaspoon white pepper

1 tablespoon ground cumin

1 tablespoon Old Bay seasoning

1 teaspoon cayenne pepper

1 teaspoon sweet paprika

1 teaspoon dried oregano

8 cups Fish Stock (page 265) or store-bought

1 pound (450 g) snow crab meat, picked over for bits of shell

1 pound (450 g) peeled Nordic shrimp

1 pound (450 g) bay scallops

1 can (10 ounces/284 g) whole shelled baby clams and their juice

2 tablespoons salted butter

3 tablespoons chopped fresh flat-leaf parsley

1 Soak the navy beans in water to cover overnight. Drain before using.

2 Heat the olive oil in a large pot over medium-high heat. Once the oil is hot, add the onions and cook, stirring occasionally, until soft and translucent, about 2 minutes. Add the garlic and cook for another 30 seconds. Add the leeks and celery and cook for another 2 minutes, until they have softened. Sprinkle in the salt, white pepper, cumin, Old Bay seasoning, cayenne pepper, paprika, and oregano and cook, stirring often, for another minute. Pour in the fish stock and bring to a boil.

3 Once boiling, pour in the drained navy beans. Reduce the heat to low, cover with a lid, and simmer for 45 to 60 minutes, until the beans are tender. Once the beans are cooked, add the crab meat, shrimp, scallops, and clams with their juice. Simmer for another 5 minutes. Remove the pot from the heat, add the butter and chopped parsley, and stir gently until the butter is melted. Serve immediately.

Meat and Poultry

Fried Chicken with Hot Pepper Maple Glaze

Serves 4

Sweet, crispy, salty, spicy, and deep-fried. This recipe ticks all the boxes. The glaze is perfect to coat the chicken but could also be used as a marinade for chicken wings. This is a special treat that we make in the summer, in a cast-iron pot outside on the fire. It's a sweet sticky mess but it's worth it!

Fried Chicken

2 cups Homemade Buttermilk (page 254) or store-bought

1 teaspoon white pepper

1 teaspoon cayenne pepper

8 skinless, boneless chicken thighs

8 cups vegetable oil, for frying

2 cups all-purpose flour

2 tablespoons cornstarch

1 teaspoon kosher salt

Flaky sea salt, for sprinkling

Hot Pepper Maple Glaze

3 cups pure maple syrup

1 jar (12.7 ounces/375 mL) bomba calabrese or your favourite hot pepper spread

1 Marinate the chicken: In a large bowl, combine the buttermilk, white pepper, and cayenne pepper and stir well. Add the chicken thighs and turn to completely coat. Cover the bowl with plastic wrap and marinate the chicken in the fridge for at least 6 hours or preferably overnight.

2 When ready to fry the chicken, make the hot pepper maple glaze: In a large saucepan, combine the maple syrup and bomba calabrese. Bring to a boil over medium-high heat and reduce the glaze by a little more than half, stirring often, until thick and sticky. You should have about 1½ to 2 cups of glaze once it is reduced. Remove from the heat and set aside.

3 Deep-fry the chicken: Line a plate with paper towel and set aside. Heat the vegetable oil in a large pot over medium-high heat until it reaches 350°F (180°C) on a deep-frying thermometer.

4 Meanwhile, in a medium bowl, stir together the flour, cornstarch, and kosher salt. Take a piece of chicken from the marinade and drop it into the flour mixture. Turn to coat the chicken all over, pressing the flour onto the chicken. Place the chicken on a plate. Repeat to coat the remaining chicken.

5 Working in batches, using metal tongs, carefully lower a few pieces of chicken into the hot oil and fry until golden brown and crunchy on both sides, 8 to 10 minutes. Transfer the chicken to the paper towel to absorb excess oil. Repeat to fry the remaining chicken.

6 Place the fried chicken in a large bowl, pour over the warm hot pepper maple glaze, and toss to coat the chicken. Season with flaky sea salt to taste.

Chicken Schnitzel

Serves 4

This recipe is a perfect example of how, with a few ingredients, basic technique, and a little elbow grease, you can make a weeknight meal spectacular. By pounding the chicken breast flat, you get a totally different result, and from there the possibilities are endless. Crispy golden-brown goodness on a plate. Serve as is or with hot sauce or Honey Mustard (page 258).

4 skinless, boneless chicken breasts, tenders removed

Kosher salt

Freshly cracked black pepper

4 cups vegetable oil, for frying

1 cup all-purpose flour

5 eggs

2 cups panko breadcrumbs

1 teaspoon flaky sea salt

For serving

Hot sauce

Honey Mustard (page 258)

1 Prep the chicken: Place the chicken breasts skinned side up on a large sheet of parchment paper and butterfly them one at a time: slice the chicken horizontally through the fattest part of the breast about three-quarters of the way through, then open it like a book. Cover with another sheet of parchment. Using the smooth side of a meat mallet or the bottom of a bottle, gently pound each breast until it is about ½ inch thick all over. Season both sides of each breast with kosher salt and pepper.

2 Heat the vegetable oil in a large Dutch oven over medium-high heat until it reaches 350°F (180°C) on a deep-frying thermometer. Preheat the oven to 250°F (120°C). Line a baking sheet with paper towel and set aside.

3 While the oil and oven are heating, bread the chicken:
Set out 3 dishes large enough to fit one butterflied chicken breast. Put the flour in the first dish. In the second dish, whisk the eggs. In the third dish, spread the panko. Working with one breast at a time, use tongs to dredge the chicken through the flour, turning to coat and shaking off the excess. Dip the floured chicken into the egg, turning to coat and letting the excess drip back into the dish. Finish with the panko, pressing the crumbs into the chicken and coating both sides.

recipe continues

4 Fry the chicken: Once the oil reaches 350°F (180°C), working with one breaded breast at a time, lay the chicken in the hot oil and fry, turning once, until golden brown and cooked through, 2 to 3 minutes per side. Remove the chicken from the hot oil and transfer to the paper towel to absorb excess oil. Season the schnitzel with flaky sea salt and place in the oven while you fry the remaining chicken.

5 Serve the schnitzel with hot sauce or honey mustard.

Boiled Chicken Stew with Dumplings

Serves 6 to 8

This is a heart-warming dish made for cold winter nights or after long autumn days spent outdoors, in the woods or on a hunt. It's all there: meat, broth, and the plumpest dumplings to soak up all that flavour. Add these spoon-drop dumplings to any of your favourite stews.

Boiled Chicken

1 (3- to 3½-pound/1.35 to 1.6 kg) whole chicken

2 carrots, cut into large chunks

3 stalks celery, cut into large chunks

1 medium yellow onion, quartered

1 leek, cut into chunks

6 garlic cloves, smashed

6 sprigs fresh thyme

5 bay leaves

1 tablespoon whole black peppercorns

1 tablespoon kosher salt

Dumplings

1½ cups all-purpose flour

1½ teaspoons baking powder

1½ teaspoons kosher salt

3 tablespoons chopped fresh flat-leaf parsley

3 tablespoons salted butter, melted

¾ cup whole milk

Chicken Stew

1 tablespoon olive oil

1 medium yellow onion, diced

2 medium carrots, peeled and diced

2 stalks celery, diced

1 leek (white and light green parts only), thinly sliced

1 teaspoon kosher salt

½ teaspoon freshly cracked black pepper

3 garlic cloves, smashed and finely chopped

2 sprigs fresh rosemary

Chicken broth (reserved)

Cooked chicken (reserved)

3 tablespoons chopped fresh flat-leaf parsley

1 tablespoon fresh thyme leaves

1 Boil the chicken: Place the chicken in a large stock pot. Add the carrots, celery, onion, leek, garlic, thyme, bay leaves, peppercorns, and salt. Cover with water and bring to a boil. Reduce the heat to medium-low to maintain a gentle boil, cover with a lid, and cook for 75 to 90 minutes, occasionally skimming the foam, until the chicken begins to pull away from the bones easily. Carefully remove the chicken from the pot and set it on a plate until cool enough to handle. Reduce the heat to a simmer.

recipe continues

2 Once the chicken has cooled, pull all the meat off the bones and set aside in the fridge. Return the bones to the pot and continue simmering the broth, uncovered, for another 3 hours. Strain the broth through a fine-mesh strainer into a large bowl. Let the broth sit for 10 minutes, then skim the fat off the top. Set the broth aside for the chicken stew. Discard or compost the chicken bones and cooked vegetables.

3 Prepare the dumpling batter: In a medium bowl, stir together the flour, baking powder, salt, and parsley. Add the melted butter and milk and mix until just combined. Set aside in the fridge while you prepare the stew.

4 Make the stew with dumplings: Heat the olive oil in a large, wide pot over medium-high heat. Once the oil is hot, add the onions, carrots, celery, leek, salt, and pepper and cook, stirring constantly, for 3 to 4 minutes, until the vegetables are bright and slightly softened. Add the garlic and cook for another minute. Add the rosemary and reserved chicken broth. Bring to a simmer and cook until the vegetables are just tender, about 10 minutes.

5 Once the vegetables are tender, add the reserved chicken meat, parsley, and thyme. Bring back to a low simmer. Drop equal-size large spoonfuls of the dumpling batter into the broth, leaving some space in between as the dumplings will expand while cooking. Cover with the lid and simmer for 12 to 15 minutes, until the dumplings are puffed and cooked through. Spoon the dumplings into bowls and ladle the stew on top.

Mom's Meat Pie with Fruit Ketchup

Makes one 9-inch pie

In Québec, tourtière has a long history and needs to be prepared a certain way with specific ingredients that vary from family to family depending on what region you live in. So, this is just a simple meat pie my mom makes, and it's *so* good. The buttery flaky crust and savoury meat filling topped with sweet fruit ketchup tastes like the holidays! Double up on the recipe and pop one in the freezer. This pie is on rotation during the winter months at my house. The homemade fruit ketchup is a beautiful match, but any ketchup works.

Pastry Dough

1¼ cups all-purpose flour

1 cup whole wheat flour

½ teaspoon kosher salt

¾ cup cold salted butter, cubed

⅓ cup + 1 tablespoon cold water

Filling

1 large skin-on russet potato

1 tablespoon vegetable oil

1 large yellow onion, finely diced

½ cup finely diced celery

2 garlic cloves, smashed and chopped

¾ pound (340 g) ground pork

¾ pound (340 g) medium ground beef

1 teaspoon kosher salt

½ teaspoon freshly cracked black pepper

¼ teaspoon celery seeds

¼ teaspoon ground nutmeg

¼ teaspoon cinnamon

⅛ teaspoon ground cloves

⅛ teaspoon ground ginger

1 egg, beaten, for brushing

Fruit Ketchup (page 261), for serving

1 Make the pastry dough: In a large bowl, stir together the all-purpose flour, whole wheat flour, and salt. Add the butter and, using a pastry cutter, cut the butter into the flour until the butter is in pea-size pieces. Add the water and use your hands or a spatula to gently mix everything together just until a dough forms and sticks together. Add more water if needed. Do not overwork the dough.

2 Turn the dough out onto a lightly floured work surface. Gently knead the dough until it forms a smooth ball. Divide the dough in half and shape each piece into a disc about 1 inch thick. Wrap each disc of dough in plastic wrap and refrigerate for at least 30 minutes or up to 3 days.

recipe continues

3 Make the filling: Coarsely grate the unpeeled potato onto a kitchen towel. Roll up the towel and squeeze to wring out as much liquid as possible. Set aside.

4 Heat the vegetable oil in a medium pot over medium heat. Add the onions, celery, and garlic and cook, stirring often, until translucent, about 5 minutes. Add the pork and beef and continue cooking until the meat is fully cooked and starting to brown, 10 to 12 minutes. Sprinkle in the salt, pepper, celery seeds, nutmeg, cinnamon, cloves, and ginger; mix well. Continue to cook, stirring frequently, for another 5 minutes. Remove from the heat and fold in the grated potato. Transfer to a baking dish and spread the filling out. Place it in the fridge to cool for about 1 hour.

5 Assemble the meat pie and bake: Preheat the oven to 350°F (180°C). Butter a 9-inch pie plate.

6 On a lightly floured work surface, roll out one dough disc into a 12-inch circle, ⅛ inch thick. Lay the dough in the prepared pie plate and gently press it against the edges of the dish. Prick small holes across the surface of the dough with a fork. Fill with the meat filling, spreading it in an even layer. Roll out the second dough disc into an 11-inch circle and lay it over the filling. Trim the excess dough with a paring knife and gently pinch and fold the dough together to seal. Brush the top with the beaten egg. Cut a few holes in the top to allow steam to escape while cooking.

7 Bake the meat pie until the filling starts bubbling up through the vent holes and the crust is golden brown, 45 to 60 minutes. Let cool for 10 minutes before cutting. Serve with fruit ketchup on the side.

8 Leftover pie can be wrapped in plastic wrap and stored in the fridge for up to 5 days or in the freezer for up to 2 months. If frozen, thaw in the fridge overnight, then let sit at room temperature for a few hours before ready to bake. Reheat the pie in a 350°F (180°C) oven for 10 to 15 minutes until heated through.

Braised Beef Short Ribs

Serves 6

Set it and forget it! Braising is a great lazy way to get amazing flavour. There's a couple of key steps to follow, but basically toss everything in the pan and get on with your life. Result? Not only fork-tender meat but a luscious sauce with no extra work.

Ask your butcher to cut the short ribs in half horizontally across the bone.

1 rack bone-in beef short ribs (about 4½ pounds/2 kg), cut in half horizontally (cut by a butcher)

Kosher salt

Freshly cracked black pepper

2 tablespoons vegetable oil

1 medium yellow onion, chopped

2 medium carrots, peeled and chopped

6 garlic cloves, smashed and chopped

1 (½-inch) piece peeled fresh ginger

4 bay leaves

½ teaspoon coriander seeds

1 cinnamon stick

2 strips of orange peel

¼ cup packed brown sugar

2 tablespoons soy sauce

4 whole star anise

6 cups beef stock

2 tablespoons cornstarch

1 Cut the short ribs into 3 sections between the bones, leaving the 2 bones with less meat on them together. This will give you 6 pieces of short ribs. Generously season the short ribs all over with salt and pepper.

2 Heat the vegetable oil in a large Dutch oven over medium-high heat. Once the oil is hot, add the ribs and sear on all sides until a nice golden-brown crust forms, 2 to 3 minutes per side. Remove the ribs from the pot and set aside.

3 Reduce the heat to medium, drop in the onions, and cook, stirring occasionally, for about 4 minutes, scraping up any browned bits from the bottom of the pot. Add the carrots and continue cooking, stirring occasionally, until slightly softened, 4 to 5 minutes. Add the garlic, ginger, bay leaves, coriander seeds, cinnamon stick, and orange peel and cook, stirring, for another minute. Finally, add the brown sugar, soy sauce, star anise, and beef stock. Stir and bring to a boil.

4 Preheat the oven to 325°F (160°C).

5 Once the broth is boiling, carefully drop in the seared short ribs. Bring to a simmer, then cover with a lid and transfer to the oven. Braise until the meat is tender and easily pulls away from the bone, 2½ to 3 hours.

recipe continues

6 Once the ribs are tender, remove them from the pot, being careful to keep the meat on the bone. Set the ribs aside on a plate and cover with foil to keep them warm.

7 Strain the broth, reserving ¼ cup in a measuring cup and returning the rest to the pot. Discard or compost the solids. Bring the broth to a boil. Stir the cornstarch into the reserved broth until smooth, then add it to the pot of broth. Whisk constantly until the sauce has thickened. Return the short ribs to the pot and reheat if needed. Divide the short ribs between plates and spoon the sauce over them.

Pan-Seared Rib-Eye Steak

Serves 1 to 2

There is something about the perfect steak that just hits the spot. Great-quality beef, heat, and salt. No marinade or spices. (Okay, sometimes a little Montréal steak spice.)

   I eat steak a couple times a year—always rib-eye, and I cook it the same way every time. The rib-eye has a lot of great-tasting fat and marbling, and I like to pan-sear it so that the flavours stay in there. You don't want all that flavour dripping to the bottom of your grill or flaming up your steak. For me, the nice crust you get from a good hard sear in a cast-iron pan can't be beat. It's even better on an open fire at the cottage.

1 (2-inch-thick) rib-eye steak (14 to 16 ounces/400 to 450 g)

Kosher salt

Freshly cracked black pepper

1 tablespoon vegetable oil

3 tablespoons salted butter

2 garlic cloves, smashed

1 sprig fresh rosemary

1 Set a wire rack over a baking sheet and set aside.

2 Generously season the steak on both sides with salt and pepper.

3 Heat the vegetable oil in a cast-iron frying pan over medium-high heat. Once the pan is very hot and the oil is just starting to smoke, add the steak and sear for 2 to 3 minutes, until a golden-brown crust forms on the bottom. Turn the steak over and sear for another 2 to 3 minutes, until a golden-brown crust has formed on the other side. Add the butter, garlic, and rosemary, reduce the heat to medium-low, and baste the steak with the melted butter for about a minute.

4 Remove the steak from the pan and place it on the wire rack. Pour the butter over the steak, tent with foil, and let rest for 10 minutes.

5 Transfer the steak to a cutting board, slice it against the grain into ½- to 1-inch-thick strips, and serve drizzled with the juices that collected underneath the steak as it rested.

Braised Beef Brisket

Serves 8 to 10

Most beef brisket in Montréal is cured and brined with a mix of "secret" spices to make Montréal's iconic smoked meat sandwiches. It's a lengthy process, and when I need a fix of smoked meat I know where to go. This brisket is slow-cooked tender and not bright pink. It's perfect for a lazy weekend get-together and makes great leftovers. And yes, it's Schwartz's.

1 (5-pound/2.25 kg) untrimmed flat-cut brisket

Kosher salt

Freshly cracked black pepper

2 tablespoons vegetable oil

1 medium yellow onion, thinly sliced

3 stalks celery, roughly chopped

2 large carrots, peeled and roughly chopped

5 garlic cloves, smashed

8 sprigs fresh thyme

4 sprigs fresh rosemary

3 bay leaves

2 tablespoons tomato paste

4 cups beef stock

2 batches Brown Butter Mashed Potatoes (page 102), for serving

1 Preheat the oven to 350°F (180°C).

2 Season the brisket generously all over with salt and pepper and set aside on the counter for 30 minutes.

3 Heat the vegetable oil in a large Dutch oven over medium-high heat. Once the oil is hot, lay the brisket in the pot and sear until golden brown on both sides, 4 to 5 minutes per side. Remove the brisket from the pot.

4 Reduce the heat to medium. Add the onions, celery, and carrots to the pot and cook, stirring occasionally, for 4 to 5 minutes, until the vegetables begin to brown. Add the garlic, thyme, rosemary, bay leaves, and tomato paste and cook, stirring constantly, for 2 more minutes.

5 Pour in the beef stock, return the brisket to the pot, and bring to a boil. Once boiling, cover with a lid and transfer to the oven. Braise the brisket for about 3½ hours, until the meat is fork-tender.

6 Cool the brisket in the liquid, covered, in the fridge overnight. Letting the brisket cool completely in the liquid allows it to soak up all the flavour, as well as cool it enough to handle and slice.

7 Once cooled, remove the brisket from the liquid. Place the pot with the liquid over high heat and gently mash the cooked vegetables in the liquid. Bring to a boil and reduce the sauce by half. Strain it through a fine-mesh strainer into a bowl. Return the sauce to the pot. Discard or compost the solids.

8 Slice the brisket crosswise against the grain into ¼-inch-thick slices and carefully return to the sauce. Heat the brisket over low heat until warmed through. Divide between plates and serve with brown butter mashed potatoes.

Roast Lamb

Serves 4 to 6

I love lamb. I love lamb! This recipe is an easy introduction into the world of lamb—simple to pull off, full of flavour, and not too lamby, if that makes sense. The mix of rosemary, garlic, and slow cooking provides the perfect bite, moist and crispy and great for any summer night. You can also slow-cook it on a barbecue spit if you have one.

1 boneless lamb shoulder (about 3½ pounds/1.6 kg)

3 tablespoons olive oil, divided

12 garlic cloves, smashed and roughly chopped, divided

¼ cup chopped fresh rosemary, divided

2 teaspoons kosher salt, divided

2 teaspoons freshly cracked black pepper, divided

For serving

Tzatziki

Tomato wedges

Thinly sliced red onions

Pita Bread (page 43) or store-bought, warmed

1 Untie the lamb shoulder and spread it boned side down on a cutting board. Drizzle the lamb with half of the olive oil and sprinkle with about half the garlic, rosemary, salt, and pepper. Massage the oil and seasonings into the meat. Flip the shoulder over and repeat with the remaining half of the olive oil, garlic, rosemary, salt, and pepper. Roll up the shoulder and tie it with butcher's twine so you have a fairly even roll. Wrap the lamb in plastic wrap and let rest in the fridge for 12 hours or overnight in the fridge. This will allow the lamb to take on all the flavours you just rubbed it with.

2 When you are ready to roast the lamb, preheat the oven to 300°F (150°C). Place a rack inside a roasting pan.

3 Pour about 2 cups of water into the pan so the drippings don't burn on the bottom. Place the lamb shoulder on the rack, transfer it to the oven, and roast, uncovered, for 3½ to 4 hours, basting with the juices from the bottom a few times while it cooks, until the lamb reaches an internal temperature of 190°F (88°C) on a meat thermometer. Replenish the water in the roasting pan as needed.

4 Increase the oven temperature to 425°F (220°C) and continue cooking for another 10 to 15 minutes, until the outside of the lamb is crispy. Remove from the oven. Leave the lamb in the pan, cover with foil, and let rest for 30 minutes.

5 Transfer the lamb to a cutting board. Using 2 forks, pull the meat into big chunks. Transfer the pulled lamb to a serving platter and serve with tzatziki, tomato wedges, red onions, and warmed pita bread.

Sugar Shack

As the snow starts to melt and the sun shines a little brighter, the days get longer, and that means maple season is around the corner. Growing up, spring meant cabane à sucre! Going to cabane à sucre is always a big production, featuring all-you-can-eat family-style Melmac sharing dishes full of Québecois classics—omelettes, oreilles de crisse, baked beans, pancakes, ham, maple bacon, pickled beets, and all of this smothered in maple syrup. After eating way too much, it's time for maple sugar pie and the star of the show, tire d'érable. In Québec this is tradition, and everybody looks forward to sugaring off.

It was my friend Cezin from Kitigan Zibi First Nation who inspired me to make maple syrup. She showed me how to tap trees, collect the maple water, and boil it to make the syrup. She also showed me how she thanks every tree and pays respect to her ancestors.

Now I make maple syrup with my boys and the family. It's not what I would call a large operation—twenty-five trees, a couple of days in the woods, and hopefully everyone gets a bottle of syrup. This sweet all-natural liquid gold may be one of our biggest exports and one of the most delicious sweeteners on the planet, but it's also a great excuse to spend some time with family and work tirelessly for a small amount of maple syrup. We get about one litre of syrup from every forty litres of sap, but it's worth it.

Tire d'érable

The best part of cabane à sucre must be classic tire d'érable, or maple taffy, boiled-down maple syrup traditionally served on snow and rolled onto sticks. I like to use crushed ice in place of snow, to guarantee a toxin-free surface.

You'll need 8 wooden popsicle sticks to roll up the maple taffy (or you can use teaspoon handles).

Crushed ice

1 can (18.25 ounces/540 mL) pure maple syrup

½ teaspoon salted butter or a small piece of bacon

1 Pack the crushed ice into a deep serving tray and keep it in the freezer (or outside, if it's cold enough) until ready to pour the hot syrup over top.

2 Pour the maple syrup into a medium pot over medium-high heat. Place a candy thermometer in the pot and boil the maple syrup until it reaches the soft-ball stage (237 to 240°F/114 to 116°C), about 20 minutes. Do not stir the maple syrup or it will crystallize. When it is done, it will be much thicker.

3 Using a ladle, pour about 2-tablespoon portions of hot syrup in a strip over the crushed ice and let it sit for a few seconds to firm up. Roll it up with a wooden popsicle stick (or the handle of a teaspoon).

Crêpes au Sirop d'érable

This is my version of the famous crêpes with maple syrup from Fairmont Le Château Montebello in Québec. It's been a family tradition for many years to meet up in Montebello for a few days during the holidays, and enjoying their crêpes is always part of our stay. I look forward to this decadent buffet item every year—rolled-up crêpes baked with a buttery maple sauce. Can you blame me? Enjoy . . . once a year!

You can make these crêpes in advance and freeze in a stack for a few weeks until ready to use. Let them sit on the counter to thaw out completely and they'll easily peel apart.

Crêpe Batter

1¼ cups all-purpose flour

1 tablespoon granulated sugar

½ teaspoon kosher salt

2 large eggs, at room temperature

2½ cups whole milk

3 tablespoons salted butter, melted and cooled slightly

1½ teaspoons pure vanilla extract

Maple Sauce

1 cup pure maple syrup

½ cup salted butter

1 Make the crêpe batter: In a large bowl, combine the flour, sugar, salt, eggs, milk, melted butter, and vanilla. Gently whisk just until the batter is smooth. Cover with plastic wrap and let the batter rest for 1 hour in the fridge. This will allow any gluten that has developed to relax, ensuring a tender crêpe.

2 Meanwhile, make the maple sauce: In a medium saucepan, combine the maple syrup and butter and bring to a simmer over medium heat. Once the mixture is simmering, remove from the heat and set aside.

3 Make the crêpes: Once the crêpe batter has rested, preheat the oven to 375°F (190°C). Have ready a 13 × 9-inch baking dish.

4 Place an 11-inch crêpe pan or a medium nonstick frying pan over medium heat and let the pan get hot. Give the batter a quick stir. Ladle about 3 tablespoons of batter into the middle of the pan. Using a crêpe spatula, spread the batter in a circular motion to cover the entire bottom of the pan. (Alternatively, ladle the batter into the pan and tilt the pan to evenly coat the bottom.) Cook for 1 to 1½ minutes, until the batter has set. Using a spatula, flip the crêpe and cook for another minute. Once the crêpe is cooked, roll it up and place in the baking dish. Repeat until all the crêpe batter is used, laying each rolled crepe beside the last.

5 Once all the crêpes are in the baking dish, pour the maple sauce evenly over top. Bake for 20 to 25 minutes, until bubbling and golden on top.

Grands-Pères au Sirop d'érable

Serves 4 to 6

These little dumplings boiled in maple syrup are traditionally eaten during *le temps des sucres*, the period in springtime when the maple sap is collected and boiled to make maple syrup. This is the simplest, most straightforward way to make your kids happy on short notice. Most items are in your pantry or fridge, it's really quick to make, and the result is spectacular. These dumplings are a little chewy, a bit fluffy, and *very* addictive. Your kids don't need to know it's this easy!

Maple Sauce

1½ cups pure maple syrup

½ cup water

Dumpling Batter

2 cups all-purpose flour

1 tablespoon baking powder

1 teaspoon kosher salt

1 tablespoon cold salted butter, cut into ½-inch cubes

1 cup whole milk

1 Make the maple sauce: In a medium braiser, combine the maple syrup and water and bring to a boil over medium-high heat. While the syrup is heating, make the batter.

2 Make the dumpling batter: In a medium bowl, stir together the flour, baking powder, and salt. Pinch the butter to form small pea-size lumps in the flour, then slowly mix in the milk with a fork until a thick batter forms.

3 Cook the dumplings: Using a soup spoon, gently drop spoonfuls of the batter into the boiling syrup. Be careful not to crowd the pot, as the batter will puff and expand. Reduce the heat to low and cook the dumplings until they are puffed and cooked through, 15 to 20 minutes, turning them over halfway through. Serve the dumplings with a generous ladleful of maple sauce.

Maple Doughnuts

Makes 12 doughnuts

Perfectly round fried balls of dough, soaked in maple syrup and topped with some maple sugar crumbs and flaky sea salt to bring it all together. My kids would eat these every weekend if they could! You can fry and soak the doughnuts in advance and take them anywhere. They are perfect served at an outdoor hockey rink with blazing hot coffee.

Doughnuts

1 cup whole milk, warmed

¼ cup granulated sugar

1½ teaspoons active dry yeast

2¼ cups all-purpose flour

½ teaspoon kosher salt

¼ teaspoon ground nutmeg

1 egg, beaten

½ cup salted butter, melted and cooled slightly

1 teaspoon pure vanilla extract

8 cups vegetable oil, for frying

Maple Soak

3 cups pure maple syrup

To finish

¼ cup maple sugar crumbs

Flaky sea salt

1 Make the dough: In a small bowl, whisk together the milk, sugar, and yeast. Let sit until the yeast begins to foam, 5 to 7 minutes.

2 In a large bowl, stir together the flour, kosher salt, and nutmeg.

3 Once the yeast is active, add the egg, melted butter, and vanilla. Add the yeast mixture to the flour mixture and mix with a wooden spoon until a dough forms. Turn the dough out onto a lightly floured work surface and knead for 5 minutes, until smooth. Place the dough in a lightly oiled bowl, cover with plastic wrap, and let rest on the counter until doubled in size, about 1 hour.

4 Prepare the maple soak: When the dough is close to doubled, make the maple soak. Pour the maple syrup into a medium pot. Bring to a boil over medium-high heat, then reduce the heat to low and simmer for 5 minutes. Remove from the heat and set aside.

5 Shape the doughnuts and deep-fry: Once the dough has risen, punch it down with your hands to remove the air. Turn the dough out onto an unfloured work surface. Using your hands, roll the dough into a log about 18 inches long and 1 inch thick. Cut the dough crosswise into 12 equal pieces. Shape each piece into a smooth ball by rolling it under the palm of your hand.

recipe continues

6 Line a plate with paper towel. Heat the vegetable oil in a large pot over medium-high heat until it reaches 350°F (180°C) on a deep-frying thermometer.

7 Working in batches so you don't crowd the pot, carefully drop 4 to 6 balls of dough into the hot oil and fry, turning occasionally, until golden brown all over, 4 to 6 minutes. Using a slotted spoon, remove the doughnuts from the hot oil and transfer them to the paper towel to absorb excess oil.

8 Finish the doughnuts: When all the doughnuts are fried, drop them into the maple soak and let them sit for about 5 minutes, turning them over a few times to coat.

9 Scoop the doughnuts out of the maple soak and place them on a serving plate. Top them with maple sugar crumbs and a bit of flaky sea salt.

Pouding Chômeur

The name says it all! Pouding chômeur literally translates as "welfare pudding." It's a decadent classic Québecois self-saucing cake that was very inexpensive and easy to make with ingredients that most people had on hand. These days, ingredients are expensive, but those needed for this recipe you likely already have at home.

Cake Batter

¾ cup all-purpose flour

1 teaspoon baking powder

1 teaspoon kosher salt

½ cup whole milk, at room temperature

1 large egg, at room temperature, beaten

6 tablespoons granulated sugar

4 tablespoons salted butter, melted

1 teaspoon pure vanilla extract

Sauce

1¼ cups heavy (35%) cream

1 cup pure maple syrup

¼ cup packed brown sugar

1 Make the cake batter: Preheat the oven to 350°F (180°C). Have ready an ungreased 9-inch square baking dish.

2 In a medium bowl, stir together the flour, baking powder, and salt.

3 In a separate large bowl, combine the milk, egg, granulated sugar, melted butter, and vanilla. Whisk until smooth. Add the wet ingredients into the dry ingredients mixing together slowly, being careful not to overmix. Pour the batter into the baking dish and set aside while you prepare the sauce.

4 Make the sauce and bake: In a medium saucepan, combine the cream, maple syrup, and brown sugar. Bring to a boil over medium-high heat, whisking constantly. Reduce the heat to low and simmer for 5 minutes.

5 Evenly and gently pour the sauce over the batter. Bake until a skewer inserted in the centre of the cake comes out mostly clean, 25 to 30 minutes. Let the pouding chômeur rest for 10 minutes before serving.

Maple Pecan Pie

Serves 8

When we opened Garde Manger in 2006, we were finally realizing our dream of owning a restaurant. After a month of renovations, we had it almost all figured out, the place looked good, and the staff was ready to go. But we had no passion for making desserts. Like a lot of cooks, we were scared by baking, pastries, desserts, and basically anything with precise measuring of ingredients. So for a while my mom made all our desserts! This is the maple pecan pie she used to make. It's a perfect mix of sweet, gooey, crunchy, and savoury.

Pastry Dough

1⅔ cups all-purpose flour

½ cup cold salted butter, cut into ½-inch cubes

1 teaspoon kosher salt

1 large egg

1 tablespoon ice water, plus more as needed

Filling

⅓ cup pure maple syrup

1 large egg

1½ cups brown sugar

½ cup heavy (35%) cream

1½ cups toasted pecans

1 Make the pastry dough: In a large bowl, mix the flour, butter, and salt. Using a pastry cutter, cut the butter into the flour until the mixture resembles coarse breadcrumbs.

2 In a small bowl, whisk together the egg and ice water. Add to the flour and, using your hands, bring the dough together until it just barely hangs together. Do not overmix. If it's too dry, add more water a tablespoon at a time, until it just comes together.

3 Turn the dough out onto a lightly floured work surface and gently knead for 2 minutes. Shape the dough into a disc, wrap with plastic wrap, and refrigerate for at least 30 minutes and up to 3 days.

4 Meanwhile, preheat the oven to 350°F (180°C).

5 On a lightly floured work surface, use a rolling pin to roll out the dough into a 12-inch circle, about ⅛ inch thick. Lay the dough in a 9-inch pie plate and gently press it against the edges of the dish. Prick small holes across the surface of the dough with a fork. Trim excess dough and crimp the edges.

6 Make the filling and bake: In a large bowl, whisk together the maple syrup, egg, brown sugar, and cream until smooth. Pour the filling into the pie shell. Spread the pecans evenly over the filling. Bake until the filling is set, about 35 minutes. Transfer to a wire rack and let cool completely before serving. Store leftover pie, wrapped in plastic wrap, on the counter for up to 2 days.

Creton

Creton is a fatty meat spread (you don't hear that often!) that's traditionally served at breakfast. It's basically Québec's version of rillettes. The best way to eat creton is on top of buttered white toast with yellow mustard, and it's even better at an old-school truck stop along one of Québec's highways.

4 tablespoons salted butter

1 medium yellow onion, diced

2 garlic cloves, smashed and chopped

1 pound (450 g) ground pork

2 teaspoons kosher salt

½ teaspoon freshly cracked black pepper

¼ teaspoon cinnamon

¼ teaspoon ground allspice

¼ teaspoon dried savory

1 cup whole milk

½ cup chicken stock

2 cups cubed white bread

For serving

Toasted white bread, buttered

Pickles

Yellow mustard

1 Melt the butter in a medium saucepan over medium heat. Once the butter is melted and bubbling, toss in the onions and garlic and cook, stirring often, until the onions are soft and translucent, 4 to 5 minutes. Add the pork, salt, pepper, cinnamon, allspice, savory, milk, chicken stock, and bread cubes and mix well. Reduce the heat to low, cover with a lid, and simmer for 1 hour, stirring every 10 minutes.

2 Remove the lid and cook until all the liquid has evaporated, about 30 minutes. Pour the creton into a terrine mould or other container. Let cool for at least 8 hours or overnight in the fridge before serving.

3 Unmould the creton, slice it, and serve with buttered toast, pickles, and mustard. Leftover creton can be stored, wrapped in plastic wrap, in the fridge for up to 1 week.

Maple Baked Beans

Serves 8 to 10

The best part about making your own baked beans is that you can control the sweetness and avoid overcooking them—totally worth the effort. A classic item on a cabane à sucre menu, baked beans are easy to make, cost-efficient, and perfect any way, sweet or savoury. These slow-cooked maple-infused beans are best on a cold winter day or at cabane in the springtime, where we add an extra drizzle of maple syrup!

4 cups dried navy beans

1 pound (450 g) thick-cut bacon, diced

2 small yellow onions, diced

¼ cup Ketchup (page 260) or store-bought

¼ cup fancy molasses

2 tablespoons brown sugar

2 tablespoons apple cider vinegar

1 tablespoon Dijon mustard

1½ teaspoons kosher salt

1 teaspoon freshly cracked black pepper

1 cup pure maple syrup

6 cups water

1 Place the beans in an extra-large container. Cover the beans with lots of cold water, leaving enough space for the beans to expand but still be covered with water. Place the container in the fridge and let the beans soak for 12 hours or overnight. Drain before using.

2 Preheat the oven to 350°F (180°C).

3 In a large Dutch oven over medium heat, cook the bacon, stirring often, until it starts to brown, 5 to 7 minutes. Add the onions and cook, stirring often, until they soften and begin to colour, about 5 minutes.

4 Add the ketchup, molasses, brown sugar, apple cider vinegar, mustard, salt, and pepper. Continue cooking for another 3 minutes, stirring constantly. Add the maple syrup, water, and the drained beans. Increase the heat to high and bring to a boil. Once it has come to a boil, cover with a lid, transfer to the oven, and bake for 2 hours, stirring every half-hour. Remove the lid and bake for another 30 minutes. Cool slightly before serving. The baked beans can be cooled completely and stored in an airtight container in the fridge for up to 5 days or in the freezer for up to 2 months.

Pea Soup with Smoked Ham

Serves 6 to 8

This soup is a classic Québecois comfort food, and every family has its own version, but all pretty much taste the same. Served everywhere from school cafeterias and hospitals to the sugar shack, our famous pea soup can be eaten as an appetizer or a main course. It's the perfect thing to warm you up on a cold winter day and gives you the fuel to keep going on the ski slopes.

2 tablespoons salted butter

1 small yellow onion, diced

2 stalks celery, diced

1 medium carrot, peeled and diced

3 large garlic cloves, smashed and chopped

1 smoked ham hock

3 bay leaves

2 sprigs fresh thyme

2 teaspoons dried savory

3 cups dried yellow split peas, rinsed

4 cups Chicken Stock (page 264) or store-bought

3 cups water

2 tablespoons kosher salt

2 teaspoons freshly cracked black pepper

1 Melt the butter in a large pot over medium-high heat. Once the butter has melted, add the onions, celery, carrots, and garlic and cook, stirring occasionally, for 5 to 7 minutes, until the vegetables are slightly softened. Add the ham hock, bay leaves, thyme, savory, split peas, chicken stock, water, salt, and pepper. Increase the heat to high and bring to a boil. Once it has come to a boil, reduce the heat to low, cover with a lid, and simmer for 2 to 2½ hours, stirring every half-hour, until the peas are soft and the soup has thickened. Discard the bay leaves and thyme sprigs.

2 Remove the pork hock, transfer to a cutting board, and let sit until cool enough to handle. Shred the meat with a fork, discarding the fat, skin, and cartilage. Return the shredded meat to the soup and stir. Reheat if needed.

3 Ladle into bowls and serve. Store leftover soup in an airtight container in the fridge for up to 4 days or in the freezer for 2 months.

Desserts

Clementine Jello

Serves 6

Clementines are a winter staple in most households. You buy a box, eat a few, toss some in school lunches for snacks, juice a few for breakfast, and you're still left with a lot. This is the perfect recipe for those not-so-fresh hardened clementines that seem never to end.

2 packets (1 tablespoon each) unflavoured powdered gelatin

4 cups freshly squeezed clementine juice (from about 32 clementines), divided

¼ cup granulated sugar

½ teaspoon vanilla bean paste

Pinch of sea salt

Seeds from 1 pomegranate, for garnish

1 Empty the gelatin packets into a medium bowl. Add 3 tablespoons of the clementine juice and stir.

2 In a small saucepan, combine 1 cup of the clementine juice and the sugar. Heat over medium heat until just warm and the sugar has dissolved. Pour the warm juice into the clementine gelatin and stir until the gelatin is fully dissolved. Pour in the remaining clementine juice, add the vanilla bean paste and salt, and stir.

3 Divide the mixture equally between 6 serving cups, cover with plastic wrap, and let set in the fridge for at least 2 hours or up to 3 days. When ready to serve, top with the pomegranate seeds.

Apple Galette

Serves 6

This is the most eaten dessert at my house—by both adults and kids. Apples are always around, they're the least exotic, most local fruit, and we love them. During apple-picking season galette is a must, but it's also good for apples that are losing their lustre. This is a great recipe to make with kids—it's free-form, so no precision is needed, and no matter how it looks, it always tastes amazing. I like using Empire apples, but any sweet baking apple will work.

Pastry Dough

1 cup all-purpose flour

1 tablespoon granulated sugar

1 teaspoon kosher salt

6 tablespoons cold salted butter, cut into ½-inch cubes

1 egg, lightly beaten

Vanilla Butter

4 tablespoons salted butter

1 vanilla bean, split lengthwise and seeds scraped out, pod reserved

Filling

¼ cup packed brown sugar

3 Empire apples, peeled, cored, and sliced about ¼ inch thick

For assembly

1 large egg, lightly beaten

2 tablespoons turbinado sugar

1 teaspoon flaky sea salt

1 Make the pastry dough: In a medium bowl, stir together the flour, granulated sugar, and salt. Add the butter and, using your hands, pinch the butter to form small pea-size lumps in the flour. Add the egg and mix in with a fork until a rough dough comes together.

2 Turn the dough out onto a lightly floured work surface and knead until smooth. Shape the dough into a small rectangle, wrap it in plastic wrap, and refrigerate for at least 30 minutes or up to 3 days.

3 Meanwhile, make the vanilla butter: Combine the butter and vanilla seeds in a medium saucepan. Cook over medium heat, stirring occasionally, until the butter has browned. Be careful not to burn it. Remove from the heat and set aside.

4 Roll out the dough: Preheat the oven to 375°F (190°C). Line a baking sheet with a silicone baking mat or parchment paper.

5 On a lightly floured work surface, roll out the chilled dough into a 16 × 12-inch rectangle (it doesn't need to be exact). Trim the edges, then lay the dough on the lined baking sheet.

recipe continues

6 Fill, finish, and bake the galette: Evenly sprinkle the brown sugar all over the dough, leaving a 1½-inch border on all sides. Arrange the apple slices evenly over the sugar, overlapping slightly. Gently fold the border of the dough up over the apples, pinching in the corners if needed to help keep its shape.

7 Drizzle the browned vanilla butter all over the apples and lay the vanilla pod pieces on top. Brush the pastry edge with the beaten egg. Sprinkle the turbinado sugar all over the pastry and apples. Sprinkle the apples with the flaky sea salt. Bake for 40 to 45 minutes, until the apples are tender and the crust is golden brown. Store leftover galette, covered with plastic wrap, on the counter for up to 2 days.

Henri's Blueberry Pie

One of our favourite activities in the summer is berry picking. Like any harvesting, it's addictive and we always come home with a lot of berries. We wash and dry them, freeze them on trays, then store for the fall and winter. When my son Henri was driving me nuts one autumn Sunday afternoon, I put him to work, and with some guidance (okay, I did most of it!) he made this masterpiece.

Pastry Dough

1½ cups all-purpose flour

1 teaspoon granulated sugar

1 teaspoon kosher salt

¾ cup cold salted butter, cubed

⅓ cup + 1 teaspoon ice water

1 tablespoon freshly squeezed lemon juice

Filling

5 cups frozen wild blueberries

Zest of ½ lemon

1 tablespoon freshly squeezed lemon juice

½ teaspoon vanilla bean paste

½ cup packed brown sugar

2 tablespoons cornstarch

¼ teaspoon kosher salt

For assembly

1 egg, beaten

1 tablespoon turbinado sugar

1 Make the pastry dough: In a medium bowl, stir together the flour, granulated sugar, and salt. Add the butter and cut it in using a pastry cutter until pea-size chunks form. Add the water and the lemon juice and gently bring the dough together using your hands.

2 Turn the dough out onto a lightly floured work surface and knead 2 or 3 times until mostly smooth. Divide the dough into 2 equal portions, shape into discs, wrap with plastic wrap, and place in the freezer for 15 minutes.

3 While the dough is chilling, preheat the oven to 350°F (180°C) and prepare the filling.

4 Make the filling: In a medium bowl, combine the blueberries, lemon zest, lemon juice, vanilla bean paste, brown sugar, cornstarch, and salt. Toss to coat.

5 Assemble and bake the pie: Butter a 9-inch pie plate. On a lightly floured work surface, using a rolling pin, roll out one portion of dough into a 12-inch circle. Lay the dough in the pie plate and gently press it against the edges of the dish. Prick small holes across the surface of the dough with a fork. Scrape the blueberry filling into the pastry shell.

recipe continues

6 Roll out the second portion of dough into an 11-inch circle. Lay the dough over the filling. Trim excess dough and pinch the edges to seal. Brush the top with the beaten egg. Sprinkle all over with the turbinado sugar. Use a sharp knife to cut a few vents in the top to allow steam to escape.

7 Bake for 40 to 45 minutes, until the crust is golden and the filling is bubbling. Cool before serving. Store leftover pie, covered with plastic wrap, on the counter for up to 2 days.

Summary Peach Cobbler

Serves 6 to 8

Eating and cooking seasonally makes a lot of sense because we get to use ingredients in their prime. In fact, you will look forward to certain dishes that only come around once a year. This cobbler is decadent, over the top, and addictive yet very simple to make. So here we are, patiently waiting for summer.

6 ripe peaches

¾ cup packed brown sugar

1 teaspoon kosher salt, divided

1 cup all-purpose flour

1 cup granulated sugar

2 teaspoons baking powder

¾ cup Homemade Buttermilk (page 254) or store-bought

1 teaspoon vanilla bean paste

6 tablespoons Brown Butter (page 255), melted

Vanilla ice cream, for serving

1 Preheat the oven to 350°F (180°C).

2 Bring a large pot of water to a boil. Cut a shallow X on the bottom of each peach then carefully drop them into the boiling water and blanch for 30 seconds. Remove the peaches with a slotted spoon and place them on a cutting board. Using a paring knife, peel the skin off the peaches. Cut the peaches in half and remove the pits. Slice each half into 4 pieces and place them in a large bowl. Add the brown sugar and ½ teaspoon of the salt and toss to coat, being careful to not break the peach slices. Set aside.

3 In a large bowl, stir together the flour, granulated sugar, baking powder, and the remaining ½ teaspoon salt. Add the buttermilk and vanilla bean paste and mix until just combined.

4 Evenly pour the melted brown butter into a 13 × 9-inch baking dish. Scrape the batter into the dish and gently spread evenly. Spoon the peach slices and any accumulated juices evenly over the batter.

5 Bake for 35 to 40 minutes, until bubbly and golden. Let cool for 5 minutes before serving. Serve with a scoop of vanilla ice cream. Store leftover cobbler, covered with plastic wrap, on the counter for up to 2 days.

Pineapple Cake with Coconut Sorbet

Serves 6 to 8

If you like piña coladas, you are going to love this combo of upside-down pineapple cake and coconut sorbet. Wintertime in Montréal is when we are faced with the cruel reality that our local fruits are not available. That's when we get tropical. My kids love virgin piña coladas, so I made them a cake version they can enjoy. Hold the rum!

Coconut Sorbet
(Makes about 4 cups)

2 cans (13.5 ounces/400 mL each) full-fat coconut milk

2 cups unsweetened coconut flakes

1 cup granulated sugar

¾ teaspoon pure vanilla extract

½ teaspoon kosher salt

Cake Topping

8 slices fresh pineapple, about ¾ inch thick, core removed

4 tablespoons salted butter, melted

¼ cup packed brown sugar

Cake Batter

1½ cups all-purpose flour

1 teaspoon baking powder

¼ teaspoon baking soda

1 teaspoon kosher salt

6 tablespoons salted butter, at room temperature

¼ cup granulated sugar

2 large egg whites, at room temperature

⅓ cup sour cream, at room temperature

1 teaspoon pure vanilla extract

⅓ cup whole milk, at room temperature

1 Make the coconut sorbet:
In a medium saucepan, combine the coconut milk, coconut flakes, granulated sugar, vanilla, and salt. Bring to a boil over high heat, stirring occasionally, then remove from the heat and let cool completely.

2 Once cooled, strain the mixture through a fine-mesh strainer into a medium bowl. Discard the soaked coconut flakes. Transfer the coconut milk mixture to an ice-cream maker and process according to the manufacturer's instructions. Transfer to an airtight container and freeze until set, at least 4 hours. Store in the freezer for up to 1 week.

recipe continues

3 Make the cake topping: Lay the pineapple slices on a few layers of paper towel for a few minutes to dry.

4 Pour the melted butter into a 9-inch round and 2-inch-deep pie dish or cake pan. Sprinkle the brown sugar evenly over the butter. Arrange the pineapple slices evenly over the sugar. Transfer the dish to the fridge while you prepare the cake batter.

5 Make the batter and bake: Preheat the oven to 350°F (180°C).

6 In a medium bowl, stir together the flour, baking powder, baking soda, and salt. Set aside.

7 In a large bowl using a hand-held electric mixer, or in a stand mixer fitted with the paddle attachment, beat the butter on high speed until smooth and creamy, about 1 minute. Add the granulated sugar and beat on high speed for another minute. Scrape down the sides of the bowl. Add the egg whites and beat until combined. Add the sour cream and vanilla and beat until combined. Scrape down the sides of the bowl. Add the dry ingredients. With the mixer running on low speed, slowly pour in the milk and mix until combined. Do not overmix.

8 Scrape the batter over the chilled topping and spread evenly. Bake for 40 to 50 minutes, tenting the pan with foil halfway through to ensure it doesn't brown before the centre has time to cook through. The cake is done when a skewer inserted into the centre comes out clean.

9 Remove the cake from the oven and let it cool in the pan for 15 to 20 minutes. Invert a serving plate over the pan, and using oven mitts, turn the pan upside down to flip the cake onto the plate. The cake should release from the pan, and you will see pineapple slices on the top. Let sit for another 15 to 20 minutes. Serve the pineapple cake with a scoop of coconut sorbet. Store leftover cake, covered with plastic wrap, on the counter for up to 2 days.

Strawberry Cake

In my family, summer means lazy days at the cottage, fishing, campfires, and strawberries, but more specifically, strawberry cake. It was my late stepfather's absolute favourite dessert. We call it strawberry shortcake, but it's not—it's more like a hybrid vanilla sponge cake, with whipped cream and ripe local strawberries. Call it what you want, it's delicious. This one's for you, Pierre!

Cake

2½ cups all-purpose flour

1½ teaspoons baking powder

½ teaspoon baking soda

½ teaspoon kosher salt

½ pound (225 g) salted butter, at room temperature

1⅓ cups granulated sugar

2 large eggs, at room temperature

1 egg white, at room temperature

2 teaspoons vanilla bean paste

1 cup Homemade Buttermilk (page 254) or store-bought, at room temperature

Strawberries

3 pints (1.5 L/6 cups) summer field strawberries, washed, dried, and hulled

2 tablespoons granulated sugar, divided

Whipped Cream

1½ cups heavy (35%) cream

3 tablespoons icing sugar, plus more for dusting

1 teaspoon vanilla bean paste

1 Make the cake: Preheat the oven to 350°F (180°C). Butter a deep 9-inch round cake pan. Line the bottom and sides with parchment paper and butter the parchment.

2 In a medium bowl, stir together the flour, baking powder, baking soda, and salt. Set aside.

3 In a large bowl using a hand-held electric mixer, or in a stand mixer fitted with the paddle attachment, beat the butter with the granulated sugar at medium speed until smooth and creamy, 3 to 4 minutes. Scrape down the sides of the bowl. Add the eggs, egg white, and vanilla bean paste and beat until light and fluffy. Scrape down the sides again. With the mixer running on the lowest speed, incorporate the flour mixture, about ¼ cup at a time until fully mixed in. Be careful not to overmix. Pour in the buttermilk and mix until combined. Scrape down the sides and bottom of the bowl with a spatula to ensure there are no lumps.

4 Scrape the batter into the prepared cake pan and spread evenly. Bake for 25 to 30 minutes or until a skewer inserted in the centre of the cake comes out clean. Let the cake cool completely in the pan.

recipe continues

5 When ready to assemble, prepare the strawberries: Place the strawberries in a large bowl. Slice enough strawberries to make about 1 cup and place them in a small bowl. Sprinkle 1 tablespoon of the granulated sugar over the sliced strawberries and toss to coat. (These strawberries will go on the first layer of the cake.) Add the remaining 1 tablespoon granulated sugar to the whole strawberries and toss to coat. (The whole strawberries will top the cake.)

6 Prepare the whipped cream: In a medium bowl using a hand-held electric mixer, whisk the cream, icing sugar, and vanilla bean paste until stiff peaks form. Set aside.

7 Assemble the cake: Once the cake has cooled, carefully remove it from the pan and place it on a cutting board. Using a long serrated knife, cut the cake in half horizontally so you have 2 even layers. Set aside the top half of the cake. Place the bottom half, cut side up, on a serving plate. Spoon about one-third of the whipped cream onto the cake and spread it in an even layer. Arrange the sliced strawberries over the whipped cream. Place the top half of the cake, cut side down, on top. Spoon the remaining whipped cream on top of the cake and use a large spoon to spread it in an even layer. Top with the whole strawberries. Dust with a bit of icing sugar and serve. This cake is best eaten right away but can be covered with plastic wrap and stored in the fridge for up to 2 days.

Chocolate Bundt Cake

Serves 8 to 10

This is my version of our favourite cake at the neighbourhood bakery Mamie Clafoutis. My classic chocolate Bundt cake has been a regular birthday cake for both my sons and me for years. It's pure chocolate, super moist, and decadent without trying too hard. If you close your eyes and think of chocolate cake, this beauty is what will pop into your head.

Cake

1 cup brewed coffee

½ pound (225 g) salted butter, at room temperature

¾ cup unsweetened cocoa powder

2 cups all-purpose flour

2 cups granulated sugar

1½ teaspoons kosher salt

¾ teaspoon baking powder

¼ teaspoon baking soda

2 large eggs, at room temperature

½ cup plain full-fat yogurt, at room temperature

2 teaspoons pure vanilla extract

Ganache

⅔ cup semisweet chocolate chips

½ cup heavy (35%) cream

1 Make the cake: Preheat the oven to 350°F (180°C). Generously butter a 12-cup (3 L) nonstick Bundt pan.

2 In a small saucepan, combine the coffee, butter, and cocoa powder. Warm over medium heat, stirring occasionally, until the butter is melted. Remove from the heat and stir until smooth. Set aside to cool for 5 to 10 minutes.

3 In a large bowl, stir together the flour, sugar, salt, baking powder, and baking soda. Add the cooled coffee mixture and mix well.

4 In a medium bowl, whisk together the eggs, yogurt, and vanilla. Add the wet ingredients to the flour mixture and mix until smooth.

5 Scrape the batter into the prepared Bundt pan and smooth the top. Bake for 45 to 55 minutes, until a skewer inserted into the centre of the cake comes out clean. Cool the cake in the pan for 5 minutes, then invert the pan onto a wire rack, leaving the pan over the cake. After 5 minutes, carefully lift the pan off the cake. (You might need to tap the bottom to dislodge the cake.) Cool the cake completely before pouring over the ganache.

recipe continues

6 Make the ganache and finish: Place the chocolate chips in a small bowl.

7 Pour the cream into a small saucepan and heat until just simmering. Once the cream is hot, pour it over the chocolate and gently stir until all the chocolate is melted and the ganache is smooth.

8 Place the cake on a serving plate. Pour the ganache over the cake. Allow the ganache to set for at least 4 hours before serving. Store leftover cake in an airtight container on the counter for up to 2 days.

Sufganiyot (Hanukkah Doughnuts)

Makes 12 sufganiyot

At my house, we celebrate Christmas and Hanukkah, or Christmukkah! We mix and match traditions and foods from both cultures and feast on a melting pot of holiday favourites. Turkey and latkes, anyone? The whole family looks forward to these doughnuts every year because they taste amazing and are a sign that the holidays are coming.

I've included our favourite fillings (lemon curd, salted caramel, and strawberry jam) for a fun mixed variety. You can choose only one filling or make all of them! Cutting corners and using store-bought fillings or chocolate spread is always an option when pinched for time. This recipe is fairly simple, don't be scared to give it a try. You can't beat homemade fresh doughnuts.

Lemon Curd

3 large eggs

1 cup granulated sugar

½ cup freshly squeezed lemon juice

4 tablespoons salted butter, cubed

Zest of 1 lemon

Salted Caramel

½ cup granulated sugar

3 tablespoons water

½ cup heavy (35%) cream, warmed

½ cup salted butter

1½ teaspoons kosher salt

Doughnuts

½ cup warm water

1½ teaspoons active dry yeast

½ teaspoon granulated sugar

1½ cups all-purpose flour, plus more for shaping the dough

2 tablespoons icing sugar, plus more for dusting

1 teaspoon kosher salt

1 large egg yolk

1 tablespoon vegetable oil

1 teaspoon pure vanilla extract

8 cups vegetable oil, for frying

1 cup strawberry jam, for filling

1 Make the lemon curd: In a medium saucepan, combine the eggs, granulated sugar, and lemon juice and whisk until smooth. Add the butter and lemon zest and cook over medium-low heat, constantly stirring, until the mixture thickens and easily coats the back of a spoon, 3 to 5 minutes. Remove from the heat and let cool completely before filling the doughnuts. The lemon curd can be stored in an airtight container in the fridge for up to 10 days.

recipe continues

2 Make the salted caramel: In a medium heavy saucepan, combine the granulated sugar and the water. Cook over medium-high heat, stirring to dissolve the sugar, but stop stirring once the sugar is boiling and begins to colour. While the sugar is browning, frequently lift the pot, carefully swirl it around, and then put it back over the heat. As soon as all the sugar is a golden-brown caramel colour, remove the pot from the heat. Carefully add the warm cream and stir until smooth. Add the butter and salt and stir until all the butter is melted and the caramel is smooth.

3 Cool the caramel in the pot, then transfer it to a container, cover, and chill in the fridge for at least 6 hours or up to 2 weeks.

4 When you are ready to fill the doughnuts, use a hand-held electric mixer, or a stand mixer fitted with the whisk attachment, to whip the caramel on high speed until fluffy and soft.

5 Make the dough and let rest: In a small bowl, whisk together the water, yeast, and granulated sugar. Let sit until the yeast begins to foam, 5 to 7 minutes.

6 In a medium bowl, stir together the flour, icing sugar, and salt.

7 Once the yeast is active, add the egg yolk, vegetable oil, and vanilla and stir until fully incorporated.

8 Add the wet ingredients to the dry ingredients and mix with a wooden spoon until a smooth dough begins to form. Using your hands, knead the dough in the bowl 4 or 5 times to form a ball. Cover the bowl with plastic wrap and let the dough rest on the counter until doubled in size, 1 to 2 hours.

9 Shape and deep-fry the doughnuts: Flour a baking sheet. Line another baking sheet with paper towel.

10 Turn the dough out onto a generously floured work surface. Using your hands, gently shape the dough into a 6 × 4-inch rectangle, adding more flour underneath as needed so it doesn't stick. Using a sharp knife, cut the dough into 12 equal pieces and place them on the floured baking sheet. Let rest for 15 minutes.

11 While the dough is resting, heat the 8 cups of vegetable oil in a large braiser over medium-high heat until it reaches 350°F (180°C) on a deep-frying thermometer.

12 Working in batches so you don't crowd the pot, drop a few pieces of dough into the hot oil. Fry until golden brown all over, about 3 minutes, turning the doughnuts halfway through. Transfer the doughnuts to the paper towel to absorb excess oil. Repeat to cook the remaining doughnuts.

13 Fill the doughnuts: Fit 3 piping bags with medium round tips. Fill one bag with the lemon curd, the second bag with the whipped salted caramel, and the third with the strawberry jam.

14 Once the doughnuts are cool enough to handle, use a small knife to poke a hole on the short side of each doughnut to create a pocket. Fill 4 doughnuts with lemon curd, 4 with whipped salted caramel, and the remaining 4 with strawberry jam. Place the filled doughnuts on a plate and generously dust them with icing sugar. The doughnuts are best eaten right away but can be stored, covered with plastic wrap, on the counter for up to 1 day.

Chocolate Pots de Crème

Makes eight 4-ounce pots de crème

I think there is a wise old saying about not bringing your kids grocery shopping, as it inevitably turns into a disaster. "Can I have this? Can I have that?" And for my kids, it's always about chocolate pudding. But my answer to them is, "No, we can't buy the pudding, but I'll make some." This is the most luxurious, rich, and decadent pudding that can be made with ingredients in your kitchen.

Ensure you make the crème fraîche in advance.

1 cup whole milk

1 cup heavy (35%) cream

4 large egg yolks

2 tablespoons granulated sugar

4 ounces (115 g) 70% semi sweet dark chocolate, finely chopped

Flaky sea salt

4 tablespoons Crème Fraîche (page 254), for serving

1 In a medium saucepan, combine the milk and cream and bring to a simmer. As soon as it reaches a simmer, remove from the heat.

2 Meanwhile, in a medium bowl, whisk together the egg yolks and sugar until smooth.

3 Slowly pour the warm milk mixture into the yolk mixture while whisking constantly. (It is important to slowly add the milk mixture so you don't curdle the eggs.) Pour the mixture back into the saucepan and cook over medium-low heat, stirring constantly, for about 5 minutes, until the custard is thick enough to coat the back of a spoon and leaves a path when you pass your finger through it. Remove from the heat.

4 Place the chocolate in a medium bowl. Using a fine-mesh strainer, strain the warm custard over the chocolate. Gently stir until the chocolate is completely melted and the custard is smooth.

5 Divide the custard equally between eight 4-ounce ramekins and chill in the fridge, uncovered, for at least 4 hours or overnight. Serve topped with a dollop of crème fraîche.

Vanilla Crème Brûlée

Makes eight 4-ounce ramekins

Vanilla is anything but plain, and this recipe is the proof. Nothing beats breaking that caramelized sugar crust—the crackling sound, the creamy soft custard, and the pure vanilla flavour makes this a favourite at my house. A fancy dessert that's simple to make, tastes amazing, and is sure to impress.

2½ cups heavy (35%) cream

2 vanilla beans, split lengthwise and seeds scraped out

6 large egg yolks

⅓ cup + 8 teaspoons granulated sugar, divided

1 Preheat the oven to 325°F (160°C). Place eight 4-ounce ramekins in a deep baking dish.

2 Pour the cream into a medium saucepan and add the vanilla bean seeds. Bring just to a simmer over medium heat. As soon as you see any movement on the surface, remove the pan from the heat.

3 Meanwhile, in a medium bowl, whisk the egg yolks and ⅓ cup of the sugar until smooth.

4 Slowly pour the hot cream over the yolk mixture while whisking constantly. (It is important to slowly add the cream so you don't curdle the eggs.)

5 Divide the custard equally between the ramekins. Pour boiling water into the baking dish to come three-quarters of the way up the sides of the ramekins. Bake until the custards are just set but jiggle slightly when you nudge the ramekins, 40 to 50 minutes.

6 Remove the ramekins from the water and place them on a wire rack to cool for at least 30 minutes. Transfer the custards to the fridge to cool completely, at least 2 hours or preferably overnight.

7 When ready to serve, remove the custards from the fridge and pat the tops dry with paper towel. Evenly sprinkle 1 teaspoon of the remaining sugar over each custard. Using a kitchen blowtorch, caramelize the sugar by passing the flame over the sugar until it melts and turns golden brown. Let the custards sit until the sugar hardens, about 1 minute, before serving.

Staples

Homemade Buttermilk

Not everyone has buttermilk in their fridge, so this is my quick alternative you can use at home.

1 tablespoon lemon juice or white vinegar

Whole milk (enough to measure 1 cup)

1 To make 1 cup of buttermilk, pour the lemon juice into a 1-cup measuring cup, then fill the rest of the measuring cup with milk. Give it a stir and let sit for 15 minutes, and you now have buttermilk.

Crème Fraîche

Makes 2 cups

Crème fraîche is a thick, tangy, rich cream. It is similar to sour cream but has silkier texture. Store-bought versions are expensive, but you can easily make it at home with only two ingredients.

2 cups heavy (35%) cream

½ cup lemon juice

1 Stir together the cream and the lemon juice in a glass jar. Loosely cover with a kitchen towel and let sit at room temperature for 24 to 48 hours, until it smells a bit nutty and has slightly thickened.

2 Line a strainer with a coffee filter or a couple of layers of cheesecloth and set it over a deep bowl. Pour the crème fraîche into the lined strainer and let drain for 4 hours. Discard the released liquid. Transfer the thickened crème fraîche to an airtight container and store in the fridge for up to 1 week.

Brown Butter

Basically, butter caramel. Just adding heat to butter changes its whole flavour profile. Slowly caramelizing butter turns it a perfect golden-brown colour and gives it a deep sweet-nutty-buttery taste.

1 pound (450 g) salted butter, cubed

1 Melt the butter in a medium saucepan over medium-high heat. Cook, stirring constantly to prevent burning on the bottom of the pot. Once you start to see lots of little, lightly browned bits, and the butter smells slightly nutty, remove from the heat. Pour the brown butter into a bowl and let it cool before using. Store, covered, in the fridge for up to 1 month.

Mornay Sauce

Mornay sauce is a Béchamel sauce with cheese. It is one of French cooking's classic sauces. Creamy, rich, and great for broiling.

4 tablespoons salted butter

1 small onion, finely diced

2 garlic cloves, grated on a microplane

½ cup all-purpose flour

1¼ cups whole milk

1 cup heavy (35%) cream

2 bay leaves

3½ ounces (100 g) aged cheddar cheese, grated

1 teaspoon kosher salt

½ teaspoon freshly cracked black pepper

⅛ teaspoon freshly grated nutmeg

1 Melt the butter in a medium saucepan over medium heat. Add the onions and cook, stirring occasionally, until soft and translucent, 2 to 3 minutes. Add the garlic and cook for another minute. Reduce the heat to medium-low, stir in the flour, and cook, stirring constantly, for 5 minutes.

2 Stir in the milk, cream, and bay leaves. Increase the heat to medium-high and bring to a boil, stirring constantly. Once the mixture is boiling and thickened, remove from the heat. Discard the bay leaves. Add the cheddar, salt, pepper, and nutmeg and stir well until the cheese is completely melted and the sauce is smooth and creamy.

Béchamel Sauce

This classic French white sauce is made by thickening milk with a roux. Great as a base for cheese sauce or pot pies.

4 tablespoons salted butter

1 small yellow onion, finely diced

1 clove garlic, minced

¼ cup all-purpose flour

2½ cups whole milk

1 bay leaf

1 teaspoon kosher salt

¼ teaspoon freshly cracked black pepper

⅛ teaspoon freshly grated nutmeg

1 Melt the butter in a medium saucepan over medium heat. Add the onions and cook, stirring constantly, until soft and translucent, 2 to 3 minutes. Add the garlic and cook for another 30 seconds. Reduce the heat to medium-low, stir in the flour, and cook, stirring constantly, for 5 minutes.

2 Stir in the milk, bay leaf, salt, pepper, and nutmeg. Increase the heat to medium-high and bring to a boil, stirring constantly. Once the sauce is boiling and thickened, remove from the heat. Discard the bay leaf.

Hollandaise Sauce

This classic emulsified butter sauce is perfect over steak or eggs Benedict. It requires attention and precision to make but is easily mastered. It is unmatched when it comes to flavour.

3 large egg yolks

1½ tablespoons freshly squeezed lemon juice

½ teaspoon kosher salt

Pinch of cayenne pepper

½ cup salted butter, melted

1 Half fill a small saucepan with water and bring to a boil.

2 In a small metal bowl that will fit over the saucepan, whisk together the egg yolks, lemon juice, salt, and cayenne pepper. Once the water is boiling, reduce the heat to low so the water is simmering, then place the bowl over the saucepan, making sure it is not touching the water. Whisk constantly until the yolks thicken and lighten in colour, 5 to 8 minutes. Remove the bowl from the heat.

3 Wet a kitchen towel and form a circle to make a well. Place the bowl in the well so the towel holds it in place. While constantly whisking, slowly stream in the melted butter. You should have a thicker sauce. Adjust seasoning as needed and serve.

Garlic Mayonnaise

Makes about 2 cups

This mayo is a special treat! I love serving it with homemade crispy golden fries. It's smooth and creamy with bite from the raw garlic. You can also use it for dips, sandwiches, or vinaigrettes.

2 eggs

1 garlic clove, finely grated

2 teaspoons Dijon mustard

½ teaspoon kosher salt

2 cups vegetable oil

1 tablespoon lemon juice

1 In a medium bowl, whisk together the eggs, garlic, mustard, and salt by hand or with a hand blender. While whisking constantly, slowly stream in the vegetable oil. Add the lemon juice and mix until the mayonnaise is smooth, about 30 seconds. The mayonnaise can be stored in an airtight container in the fridge for up to 4 days.

Honey Mustard

This honey mustard is my go-to last-minute peacemaker sauce for my kids. Easy, tangy, sweet, and good on almost everything.

½ cup Dijon mustard

½ cup liquid honey

1 teaspoon apple cider vinegar

A pinch of sea salt

Freshly cracked black pepper

1 In a small bowl, whisk together the mustard, honey, apple cider vinegar, salt, and pepper until smooth. Store in an airtight container in the fridge for up to 1 year.

Tartar Sauce

This tartar sauce is great with fried fish, crabcakes and sandwiches. It's a step ahead of just plain mayo and relish, is less sweet, and has more vibrant flavours and a bit of crunch.

1 cup mayonnaise

½ cup plain full-fat Greek yogurt

Zest and juice of 1 lemon

2 tablespoons minced capers

2 tablespoons finely diced gherkins

2 tablespoons finely diced red onion

2 tablespoons finely chopped fresh flat-leaf parsley

2 tablespoons finely chopped fresh dill

½ teaspoon freshly cracked black pepper

1 In a medium bowl, combine the mayonnaise, yogurt, lemon zest and juice, capers, gherkins, red onion, parsley, dill, and pepper. Mix well. Store in an airtight container in the fridge for up to 1 week.

Apple Pudding

This is a fall classic at my house. Apple picking is a fall tradition, along with having too many apples. This is a great way to get rid of bruised or banged-up apples. I like using Golden Delicious apples, but you can use any variety. My apple pudding is great for a quick last minute dessert or snack.

12 apples

⅓ cup water

2 teaspoons pure maple syrup

1 teaspoon lemon juice

½ teaspoon cinnamon

A pinch of sea salt

1 Peel the apples, leaving a bit of skin on for colour. Core the apples and cut into big chunks.

2 In a medium saucepan, combine the apples, water, maple syrup, lemon juice, cinnamon, and salt. Bring to a boil over high heat, then reduce the heat to low, cover with a lid, and simmer until softened, about 20 minutes.

3 Transfer the softened apples and any juices to a food processor and quickly pulse to desired consistency, depending on how chunky you like it. (I like to blend on high speed for about 2 minutes until I get a really silky smooth texture almost like pudding.) Pass the applesauce through a sieve into a medium bowl to remove any skin. Chill in the fridge before serving. Store in an airtight container in the fridge for up to 1 week.

Pesto

Pesto can be made with a variety of leafy greens or even some vegetables. I keep nuts out of this recipe to be safe when the kids have friends over for supper.

4 cups lightly packed basil leaves

½ cup grated Grana Padano cheese

2 garlic cloves, grated on a microplane

Zest and juice of ½ lemon

½ teaspoon kosher salt

½ teaspoon freshly cracked black pepper

½ cup olive oil

1 In a food processor, combine the basil leaves, cheese, garlic, lemon zest and juice, salt, and pepper. Pulse to roughly chop. With the machine running, stream in the olive oil and blend until smooth. Serve immediately or store in an airtight container in the fridge for up to 5 days.

Ketchup

Makes about 2 cups

Sometimes I like to play with the classics. It's easier to reach into the fridge and grab ketchup, but occasionally it's fun to switch it up and go a more natural route. With great taste and definitely more texture, this ketchup is terrific on burgers, fries, and meatloaf.

1 can (5.5 ounces/156 mL) tomato paste

1 cup water

½ cup white vinegar

½ cup packed brown sugar

1 pear, cored and grated on a microplane

1 teaspoon kosher salt

½ teaspoon freshly cracked black pepper

½ teaspoon garlic powder

½ teaspoon onion powder

⅛ teaspoon ground cloves

Dash of hot sauce

1 In a small saucepan, combine the tomato paste, water, white vinegar, brown sugar, pear, salt, pepper, garlic powder, onion powder, cloves, and hot sauce. Bring to a simmer over medium-high heat and cook for 5 to 10 minutes, stirring occasionally, until slightly thickened. Remove from the heat and let cool. Store in an airtight container in the fridge for up to 1 year.

Fruit Ketchup

Makes about 4 cups

This homemade ketchup reminds me of eating at my grandmother's house. Sweet and crunchy, it goes with everything. Whether she made the fruit ketchup herself or it was store-bought, I don't know, but it was always around. Maybe that's a grandma thing.

1 tablespoon vegetable oil

1 large yellow onion, roughly chopped

2 stalks celery, roughly chopped

2 garlic cloves, smashed

2 tomatoes, roughly chopped

2 pears, cored and roughly chopped

¼ cup white vinegar

¼ cup water

¼ cup packed brown sugar

1 teaspoon ground pickling spice

½ teaspoon kosher salt

½ teaspoon freshly cracked black pepper

1 Heat the vegetable oil in a medium saucepan over medium-high heat. Add the onions, celery, and garlic and cook, stirring frequently, until softened, about 5 minutes. Add the tomatoes, pears, white vinegar, water, brown sugar, pickling spice, salt, and pepper. Bring to a boil, then reduce the heat to low and simmer for 15 minutes, stirring every so often. The fruit ketchup should be chunky and still a bit crunchy. Let cool completely. Store in an airtight container in the fridge for up to 3 months.

Roasted Tomatoes

Serves 4

Roasting tomatoes in the oven really brings out the flavours, adds some sweetness, and just takes tomatoes to the next level. Everything comes together with the olive oil and garlic.

25 cherry tomatoes

2 garlic cloves, smashed

½ cup olive oil

4 sprigs fresh thyme

½ teaspoon flaky sea salt

A few cracks of black pepper

1 Preheat the oven to 425°F (220°C).

2 In a 13 × 9-inch roasting pan, combine the tomatoes, garlic, olive oil, thyme, flaky sea salt, and pepper and gently toss together. Roast for 15 to 20 minutes, until the tomatoes have softened.

3 Set the oven to broil and cook for another 3 to 4 minutes, until lightly charred. Remove from the oven and let the tomatoes cool in the pan for at least 20 minutes. Use, or cool completely, transfer to an airtight container, and store in the fridge for up to 4 days.

Pickling Liquid

This is a universal pickling liquid that can be used for any vegetable. Use to make my Pickled Jalapeños and Pickled Ramps.

1½ cups apple cider vinegar

1 cup water

3 garlic cloves, smashed

2 tablespoons kosher salt

1 tablespoon granulated sugar

1 teaspoon coriander seeds

1 teaspoon fennel seeds

1 teaspoon whole black peppercorns

1 In a medium saucepan, combine the apple cider vinegar, water, garlic, salt, sugar, coriander seeds, fennel seeds, and peppercorns. Bring to a boil over high heat. Remove from the heat and use to pickle jalapeños or ramps (recipes below).

Pickled Jalapeños

18 to 20 jalapeño peppers, stems removed, sliced into ⅛-inch-thick rounds

1 batch Pickling Liquid, hot (recipe above)

1 Place the sliced jalapeños in a 4-cup mason jar. Cover the jalapeños with the hot pickling liquid, screw on the lid, and let sit for at least 6 hours and ideally overnight before using. The pickled jalapeños can be stored in the fridge for up to 2 months.

Pickled Ramps

1 pound (450 g) ramps, cleaned, trimmed, and leaves removed

1 batch Pickling Liquid, hot (recipe above)

1 Place the ramp bulbs in a 4-cup mason jar. Cover the ramps with the hot pickling liquid, screw on the lid, and let sit for at least 6 hours and ideally overnight before using. The pickled ramps can be stored in the fridge for up to 2 months. (The ramp leaves can be used to make pesto, page 259.)

Stocks

White Chicken Stock

Makes about 4 cups

Making stock is the best way to get the most value and flavour from a chicken. Stock is a wonderful base for so many dishes, so make it in advance and keep it frozen until needed. Freeze chicken bones until you have enough to make a stock.

3 pounds (1.35 kg) chicken bones

2 stalks celery, roughly chopped

2 medium carrots, roughly chopped

2 medium yellow onions, roughly chopped

6 sprigs fresh thyme

5 bay leaves

1 tablespoon whole black peppercorns

10 cups cold water

1 In a large stock pot, combine the chicken bones, celery, carrots, onions, thyme, bay leaves, and peppercorns. Pour in the water. Bring close to a boil, then reduce the heat to maintain a constant simmer and cook, uncovered and without stirring, for 6 hours. Skim the foam off the top every so often.

2 Strain the stock into a large bowl and let sit for 10 minutes. Once it has settled, skim off the layer of fat on the top. Use, or cool completely, then store in an airtight container in the fridge for up to 1 week or in smaller containers in the freezer for up to 3 months.

Note: For dark chicken stock, with more depth of flavour, use roasted bones: Spread the chicken bones in a roasting pan and roast in a 400°F (200°C) oven for 20 to 25 minutes, until golden brown. Transfer the bones to the stock pot. Deglaze the roasting pan over medium-high heat with about 2 cups of the water, scraping up the browned bits from the bottom, and add the deglazing liquid to the stock pot. You can also roast the vegetables first for even more flavour. To intensify the flavour even more, boil the strained stock until reduced by half.

Fish Stock

Homemade fish stock adds amazing seafood flavour to chowders, soups, and sauces. Keep frozen to use when needed.

Vegetable oil

1 medium yellow onion, roughly chopped

1 leek, roughly chopped

2 stalks celery, roughly chopped

4 garlic cloves, smashed

2 pounds (900 g) white fish bones, heads and gills discarded, cut into large pieces and rinsed

4 sprigs fresh parsley

4 sprigs fresh thyme

1 tablespoon fennel seeds

1 tablespoon whole black peppercorns

10 cups cold water

1 Heat a splash of vegetable oil in a large stock pot over medium-high heat. Add the onions, leek, celery, and garlic and cook, stirring constantly, until the vegetables are soft and translucent, 3 to 4 minutes. Add the fish bones, parsley, thyme, fennel seeds, and peppercorns. Pour in the water. Bring to a boil, then reduce the heat to maintain a constant simmer and cook, uncovered and without stirring, for 1 hour.

2 Remove from the heat and let steep for about 30 minutes. Strain the stock and use, or cool completely, then store in an airtight container in the fridge for up to 1 week or in smaller containers in the freezer for up to 2 months.

Veal Stock

Veal stock is the base for most great sauces. Roasting the bones to perfection adds great flavour and colour to the stock and is the most important step. Let the stock simmer slowly without boiling and the result is a deep-flavoured, clear, dark broth that can be used for soups and sauces. Keep in the freezer and use when needed.

4 pounds (1.8 kg) veal bones (mix of knuckle and marrow bones)

¼ cup tomato paste

2 medium yellow onions, roughly chopped

3 large carrots, roughly chopped

4 stalks celery, roughly chopped

Vegetable oil

10 bay leaves

2 tablespoons whole black peppercorns

10 sprigs fresh thyme

5 sprigs fresh rosemary

5 quarts (20 cups) cold water

Note: To make demi-glace, simmer the veal stock over medium heat until reduced to about one-third of what you started with. You'll know it's finished when it coats the back of a spoon and is sticky. It can be served with roasts or grilled steak or used as a base for sauces.

1 Preheat the oven to 400°F (200°C).

2 Spread the veal bones in a large roasting pan and roast on the top rack of the oven for 25 to 30 minutes, until they begin to brown. Remove from the oven and use a spoon to smear the tomato paste over the bones. Return the bones to the oven and roast for another 15 minutes.

3 Meanwhile, toss the onions, carrots, and celery with a bit of vegetable oil and spread them out on a baking sheet. Roast the vegetables on the lower rack of the oven for 15 to 20 minutes, until they are browned. Add to the stock pot.

4 Transfer the bones to a large stock pot. Deglaze the roasting pan over medium-high heat with 2 cups of the water, scraping up the browned bits from the bottom, and add the deglazing liquid to the stock pot.

5 Add the bay leaves, peppercorns, thyme, and rosemary to the stock pot. Pour in the remaining water. Bring to a boil, skimming the foam off the top as it forms, then reduce the heat to low and simmer, uncovered and skimming occasionally, for at least 6 hours and up to 8 hours.

6 Strain the stock and let sit for about 10 minutes. Once it has settled, skim off any gathered fat from the surface. Use, or cool completely, then store in an airtight container in the fridge for up 1 week or in smaller containers in the freezer for up to 2 months.

Acknowledgments

Cue the skunky bass line—it's time for some crucial thanks.

First, I have to give major props to Sabrina, my girlfriend and baby mama (I don't see a ring on my finger!?!) for always putting our family first. Keeping us three kids in line, doing the important work in the shadows so everything comes together, and crossing things off that famous list! It's not easy to get me to sit still for more than five minutes, so keep trying. LOL. So Big Mama, CEO of our lives, THANK YOU for all the million things that nobody sees, the emails, the doctor's appointments (I break a limb every five weeks), and everything that keeps our family afloat.

Christopher Merrick, the Merrickle Man, the Sudbury Sensation . . . or just good old BooBoo. He started working at the restaurant in 2015 and hasn't looked back. He basically took over my position, kicked me out, and has taken the restaurant to new heights. As the chef de cuisine at Garde Manger, his list of tasks ranges from psychologist to amateur plumber to accountant, and he's been taking it in stride—but is probably one burst pipe away from an aneurysm. He's always been reliable, hard-working, and extremely organized, and oh yeah, he also makes great food. He has worked relentlessly on this book with me while keeping the restaurant running better than ever. So, Chris, THANK YOU!

Marc-André Lavoie, or McD, my partner in crime for the past thirty years. We met in high school, grade nine to be exact. He was wearing John Lennon glasses, a purple jacket, and a tie with hearts and peace signs. I was wearing an Exploited T-shirt (it's a band) under my school uniform, and my general attitude was, well, basically, FTW, so yeah, a match made in heaven.

We became fast friends and realized that we were complete opposites with a lot in common. So here we are decades later, and it still feels like we're in ninth grade. We've worked on *everything* together—pictures, stickers, TV shows, social media—and through all that, we've managed to stay best friends and talk almost every day. He shot the photography for this book over a span of almost a year. It was a lot of hard work, and frustrating at times, but we pushed through, adjusting lights, changing angles, and staring at food for way too long, but we had fun doing it and got some pretty good leftovers. So McD, THANK YOU!

Ronald Lavoie—Nobody was more excited to see this book come to life than "Ronnie." He supported me when I started cooking by hiring me for special dinners at his golf club and was always the first to get the newest and best technology for his son, Marc-André, to hone his craft. He had a big personality, great sense of humour, and was not afraid to tell you what he thought. Here's to you Ronnie. RIP.

Big thanks also to:

John Withenshaw, my long-time manager who passed away this year. Nobody had more faith in me than he did. Treated me like a son and had my back through thick and thin. Nobody would've been more excited to promote this book than him. RIP.

Pierre Hébert, my stepdad of over thirty years, who we lost while writing this book. We couldn't be more different. He was a very accomplished lawyer and a great guy, but he couldn't even cook an egg! He was one of my biggest supporters and has had a huge influence on my life. One of the most ethical, honest, and heartfelt people you could ever meet. I was lucky to have him in my life. RIP.

Chuck Hughes Sr. My dad passed away at a young age when I was ten years old. He always lit up every room he walked into, was talented beyond belief in any sport he practised, and even though he left us too early, his legacy lives on every time I look in the mirror. I know he would have been proud of his little pork chop. Party on, Dad. RIP.

Big thanks to everyone at the restaurant. The only reason *Chuck's Home Cooking* exists is because there is a dedicated team of outstanding individuals that hustle at the restaurant day in and day out. After seventeen years, our little pirate ship has gone through many ups and downs, recessions, hipster invasions, and even a pandemic. But through thick and thin, we've had some of the best staff come through the doors of our humble establishment. Whether it's front of the house, kitchen staff, dishwashers, bus people, suppliers, plumbers, and so on—and of course all our loyal customers—all have played a key role in our success. Huge thanks to everybody who's been a part of it! Let's keep it loud, salty, and dark for another seventeen years.

Catherine, Gianni, and Émiliana from Ramacieri Soligo, for all the plates, dishes, and props! And for all the play dates to keep my kids out of the house so we can finally get that shot. You are great neighbours and even better friends.

Big thanks to my mom. She pushed me to cook at a time when cooking was not "cool" or even a career option in school. She had a vision, and somehow it came true. Thanks for believing in me when it was hard for me to believe in myself. Sorry for all the sleepless nights, the trips to the hospital, and every time you bailed me out of sticky situations. Love you.

Big thanks to my kids, Charles and Henri. Thank you for teaching me how to be patient, to be in the moment, and to live life to its fullest. I love you both more than words can convey. To see you grow up and become "people" has been my greatest joy and also my toughest gig. It hasn't been easy, and if I look at what I put my mom through . . . I'm in for a wild ride. Love you, boys, now go to bed.

Index